# THE WALDORF SCHOOL
# APPROACH TO HISTORY

*by*

WERNER GLAS

*Professor of Education*
*Waldorf Institute of Mercy College*

THE ANTHROPOSOPHIC PRESS

Spring Valley,                    New York

Copyright © 1963 by Werner Glas

Revised edition 1981, published and distributed by The Anthroposophic Press, 258 Hungry Hollow Road, Spring Valley, N.Y. 10977.

International Standard Book Number 0-88010-004-4

Cover design by Peter van Oordt

*Printed in the United States of America*

# THE WALDORF SCHOOL
# APPROACH TO HISTORY

# Contents

*Introduction* ............................ v

I A Contrast of Aims and Methods ............ 1

II History and Geography .................... 9

III The History of Civilization ................ 15

IV Methods of Teaching ..................... 44

V In the Quest of Images From Plutarch
to Bryant ............................. 52

VI The Seventh Grade and the Calyx of
Modern Consciousness ..................

VII The Grade Eight Curriculum: From
Copernicus to the Present ................ 70

VIII History in the High School ................ 89

# Introduction

This account of history teaching in Waldorf schools is intended for parents, teachers and the general reader interested in education. The book is also addressed to shapers of educational policy and all those who want to take a closer look at an important aspect of Waldorf education. There are compelling reasons for a reappraisal of the role of history teaching in *all* schools. Educators and historians should give watchful attention to the conservation, transmission and renewal of culture. The purpose of history lessons in elementary and secondary schools deserves more earnest thought than it usually receives.

One of the distinguishing features of this introduction to history teaching is that it deals with ideas that have been put to the test in many classrooms for decades. It is based on the achievements of the rapidly growing Waldorf school movement. Anyone setting out to write about history in the context of a living school movement naturally leans on other people's shoulders, and I have leaned on a good many. My debt to others is great.

It would require more than a brief mention of distinguished persons to recognize the many valued colleagues and consulted authors who have influenced this work, and then, too, such a list would be tediously long. So I thank them all together—the living, and those who have left the earth—for their help. One advantage of expressing gratitude in this way is that it is less likely that they are associated with my errors. The responsibility for any sins of omission, as well as the responsibility for mistakes, is mine alone.

Yet there is one fundamental indebtedness, so much greater than all the rest that it must be mentioned, although it is to a man who died before I was born. But for the work of Rudolf Steiner, the founder of Waldorf education, whose thought remains a continuing source of inspiration after thirty years of study, the important work this book describes would not exist. Steiner developed a new child psychology and related the school curriculum to child development. He shaped an art of education based on insights into the nature of the developing human being. Moreover, he *personally* guided the practical implementation of his educational philosophy, involving himself in all the practical details of a large school that has become something of an example for more than two hundred other schools. His educational thought is expressed in twenty three lecture cycles, in the recorded discussions that took place during the faculty meetings of the first Waldorf School in Stuttgart, and in many addresses to teachers, parents and the general public in Germany, Switzerland, England, Holland and the Scandinavian countries. Scattered throughout the above, Steiner left general and specific indications on history teaching that are profound and plentiful. At the same time, it is characteristic of Steiner's way of working that his lectures and writings contain seeds of a systematic philosophy of history and history teaching rather than the final formulation of one. As an educator he was interested in stimulating creative work and not in making final statements. This book is also more concerned with characterization than definition. It should be read as an introduction and not as a final statement on the subject.

One of Rudolf Steiner's major aims was to achieve a unity of experience—a balance between the sciences, the humanities and the arts. He gave special attention to the structure of the curriculum from this point of view. Steiner opposed fragmentation and did away with the kind of timetable that abruptly leaps from subject to subject. He regarded staccato transitions from one short lesson to another as a detriment to the pupil participation necessary for real learning. From the beginning he advocated the so-called "main lesson," a period that occupies the first two hours each morning. The main lesson is devoted to one subject for three, four, or even five weeks at a time. In such a time span the teacher can give proper attention to the dynamics of teaching; he can effectively build a growing sense of discovery and understanding from day to day.

The main lesson also extends concentration. It is a valuable tool for obtaining a penetrating focus on a subject of significance. Such a two-hour span can be given a wonderful form that makes it possible to achieve concentration and economy in teaching.

The well-known historian, Stewart Easton, reflecting

on *The Waldorf School Approach to History*, once wrote: "The simple magnitude of the curriculum is astonishing enough. Not only does it seem that he (the student) has to study every period of history and every major civilization in his grade school years, but he repeats it again in high school, though in an entirely different manner." This great scope of the curriculum is probably only possible because of the main lesson system, and all the history teaching described takes place in main lessons.

Much thought and effort is spent by Waldorf teachers in faculty meetings and during lesson preparation time to ensure that the main lesson appeals to different levels of experience. All education affects the conscious, the semiconscious and the unconscious life of the child. It is axiomatic for Waldorf teachers that a thing that is only known by the head is only partly known, and time is required before a real feeling for a subject takes root in a child. Such time is in part used for pertinent musical experiences, for the painting of related pictures, for relevant recitations or little plays and other artistic activities. Each morning the teacher appeals to the thinking, feeling and willing of the children. During one main lesson he brings about a movement of his theme from heart to hand and from heart to head. In order to regulate this inner dynamic the teacher must be free to shape his lessons and cannot rely on general preformulations of subject matter. Visitors notice the absence of textbooks. They may see readers, source materials, artistic illustrations, but not textbooks, as the good Waldorf teacher avoids them altogether. As A. C. Harwood wrote in *Portrait of a Waldorf School*:

> The teacher does not read to the children out of a book even when he is teaching them a poem—he knows it by heart; and the lesson is often a conversation, with teacher and children talking together about the world. In every child's desk there are notebooks: in the elementary classes, dealing with simple arithmetic and reading material; in the upper grades, dealing with such subjects as physics, chemistry, mathematics, history, geography, physiology and grammar. It is evident that much care is taken with these books—they are really texts created by the children themselves. They contain stories, poems, problems, reports on experiments, and so on, and are finely illustrated with colored diagrams and pictures.

Even notes are used sparingly or not at all because they easily can become a communication barrier. A Waldorf teacher likes to stand and move freely as he develops his lesson. His goal is to see to it that the class is truly immersed in history. The children work because they grow enthusiastic and not because they are to be graded or ranked according to an examination. There are neither grades nor examinations. Instead history is allowed to speak as a humanizing force.

Many readers are likely to be conversant with other aspects of the life work of Rudolf Steiner. They know that education is only one aspect of his many-sided work. Probably his greatest achievement was the establishment of a science of consciousness development called anthroposophy. He worked tirelessly to bring about cultural and spiritual renewal through this science. I have frequently been asked to comment on the relationship between anthroposophy, Steiner's contribution to the understanding of history, and history teaching in Waldorf schools. As this question is very much alive, and as it also helps to delineate the scope and limitations of this study, it is right to respond to it here. In order to do so, however, it is necessary to sort out a variety of activities that are commonly grouped together under the single semantic umbrella of one word—"history."

Hegel in his *Philosophy of History* had already divided the nature of historiography into three categories. He distinguished between *original history*, the work of finding archaeological artifacts, or of researching public monuments and inscriptions, or of studying documentary sources such as official documents, letters, diaries, and other items of evidence; *reflective history*, which is concerned with the effort of shaping materials into a coherent narrative and interpreting their significance; and *philosophical history*, which has something to say about the greater meaning of the historical process.

It is unusual for a Waldorf teacher to be active in the fact finding disciplines of original history, although some direct experience of historical investigation is of considerable value to the high school history specialist. Nevertheless, both class teacher and high school specialist are more concerned with the selection of facts, the way they are ordered, and how they are interpreted than with the establishment of new data. Thus, in quite different ways their main task belongs to *reflective history*. It is nothing less than creating a synthesis of historical evidence and forming imaginative presentations that give voice to the past. The teacher's ability to form living pictures and historically accurate representations can be much enhanced by exercises belonging to an anthroposophical schooling of cognition.

Disciplines for the further development of cognitive faculties are described in *Knowledge Of The Higher Worlds and Its Attainment*, as well as in many other books and lectures. These can strengthen the visual imagination as well as cultivate a sense for form akin to the artistic mastery of musical composition. A teacher following such a path is likely to be more effective in the classroom, but he will take care that his lessons remain free from concepts of philosophical history, or meta-history, as Toynbee calls it.

Reflections about history creating a philosophical or psychological or sociological framework of reference are strictly avoided in the elementary school. The conceptual element plays a greater role in high school, but usually the anthroposophical perspective of history is omitted.

It is comforting to note that Rudolf Steiner was at home in all three categories of historiography. From 1890 to 1897 he worked at the Goethe-Schiller Archieve in Weimar. During those years he edited six volumes of Goethe's scientific writings. Some of the material included in the morphological section of this great, comprehensive Goethe edition had never been published previously. While in Weimar, Steiner also edited the complete works of Schopenhauer for Cotta, and wrote a biographical introduction for this twelve-volume enterprise. He also made a selection of the writings of Jean Paul in eight volumes and of the poetry of Uhland in three. Steiner was no stranger to historical research. He also moved among many noted historical scholars: Hermann Grimm, Erich Schmidt, Wilhelm Scherer, Julius Wahle, Eduard von den Hellenen, Otto Harnack, Eugen Duhring and Heinrich von Treitschke to name only a few.

Between the ages of forty-two and sixty-three Steiner gave several hundred lectures that could be classified as *reflective history*. Interesting as some of these are, they do not constitute his main contribution. Without any doubt, Steiner's greatest and most original work belongs to the realm of philosophical or meta-history. Indeed, the extent and significance of this contribution has not yet been properly assessed. Lesser meta-historians, like Spengler and Toynbee, have received more attention. Spengler was one of the first to insist that philosophy must concern itself with history. "All genuine historical work is philosophy, unless it is mere ant-history," he wrote in *The Decline of the West*. For Spengler the historical process was like a biological cycle, an immutable and recurrent organic motion of genesis, growth, maturity, decay and death. Arnold Toynbee, less given to biological metaphor, and

assisted considerably by a classical education, soon
departed from historical determinism, which interested
him at the time he began his study of the rise and fall of
civilizations. By volume six of his monumental work he
had reached quite other conclusions. He then saw
religious experience as the central force in the development of civilizations. Religion as a creative power plays a
larger and larger role in each subsequent volume. Finally,
Toynbee describes himself as a "creationist," one who
explains civilizations in terms of religion.

For Steiner the evolution of the individual human spirit
is the focus of history. He is always, however, equally
concerned with the relationship between the one and the
many, between man and humanity.

A central thesis of the anthroposophical view of history is
that the intellectual capacities natural to the contemporary
human being have evolved from earlier modes of consciousness that brought direct experiences of transcen-
dental realities of which Steiner spoke. He regarded it as a
first requirement—that the clarity and objectivity acces-
sible to the modern mind be carried into new disciplines of
perception he called Imagination, Inspiration and Intui-
tion. For Steiner these refinements of consciousness needed
to be developed for the sake of the future needs of humanity. This area of his work is recorded in many volumes and
is most rewarding for any adult interested in the purposes
of history. Among the many starting points for such a
study *The Spiritual Guidance of Man and Humanity* leads into

the heart of the subjects. For philosophically inclined persons, *Riddles of Philosophy* is an equally good starting point.

It is of great consequence that the kind of spiritual scientific research Steiner and some others like Emil Bock completed was firmly grounded in conscious adult self-education. He stressed that neither anthroposophical research nor its findings should be taught to children. Before the age of maturity it is important to develop practicality, common sense and a mastery of the ordinary consciousness. For this reason Steiner's philosophical history has consciously been omitted from this book. It deserves a separate study, which probably will require more space than this one.

There is one other area of limitation that needs to be mentioned. Just as history grew out of a prehistoric period in which mythology played a formative part, so the child in his own consciousness recapitulates the path of humanity. Rudolf Steiner, who knew Haeckel personally, explored the relevance of the theory of recapitulation for education. Steiner did not subscribe to it in all its aspects but found some merit in it. He described one of the general developmental changes as taking place just prior to the fifth grade and indicated how a child's experience of time is quite different before and after the fifth grade. Steiner advised that history teaching proper should begin at this time. From a practical point of view the distinction between mythology and history in the elementary middle school classroom is more theoretical than actual. It is essential for any understanding of the history of civilizations to have some acquaintance with those works, both written and oral, that men felt, revered and lived. For in times past, mythologies were inextricably interwoven with the whole fabric of everyday life to an extent beyond anything in our experience.

In Waldorf schools the teaching of history is preceded by literature and language experiences that can be considered, from a purely pedagogical point of view, as related to history teaching. In the first grade fairy tales are narrated. In such stories the child can meet the forces of good and evil in an imaginative way. Later, many forms of goodness and evil appear in history. In grade two legends and fables are told and studied. In the third grade the story of creation according to Genesis is introduced. Old Testament studies include the heroic figures of spiritual leaders like Abraham, Moses, Solomon and David. In the array of seers, patriarchs, judges, kings and prophets the time sequence becomes more important than in earlier years. An additional step toward history teaching takes place. The fourth grade curriculum contains the dramatic world of Norse mythology and the Twilight of the Gods. Mythology continues into the fifth grade and beyond it. Once the fifth grade is reached, however, there is also a separate teaching of history, which is the theme of this book. The earlier mythology curriculum is not discussed but receives extensive treatment in my *Speech Education in the Primary Grades of Waldorf Schools*.

Like most things, this book also has a history. It first appeared in 1963 and was written for a conference on history teaching sponsored by Highland Hall, the oldest Waldorf school in California. The first edition became unobtainable rather rapidly, partly because many copies were stored in an unfortunate place and were eaten by termites! An unrevised second edition, published by the Waldorf Institute of Mercy College has been used by quite a number of people. Some of these have had the kindness to write to me suggesting additions and improvements. This third edition has profited from their comments. The original study has been significantly augmented. The original text is still there, but in some ways enlargement has almost made it a new work.

For the last twenty years it has been my privilege to work with a great variety of gifted people training to be Waldorf teachers. To them this effort is dedicated.

Werner Glas

Waldorf Institute of Mercy College
Southfield, Michigan
October, 1980

# I

# A Contrast of
# Aims and Methods

Among the central ideas of the twentieth century, two often appear in conflict with each other—the idea of nationalism and the concept of the unity of mankind. Nationalism, as such, was not an idea originating in our century, and yet it has reached new dimensions of power as it has spread to nearly all peoples. Perhaps equally far reaching, and certainly more distinctive of the twentieth century, is the growing view of mankind as one. We are still far from recognizing that the welfare of all is the concern of all. A maturing awareness of the *globalness* of human affairs, however, begins to permeate both the popular consciousness and serious historical scholarship. Co-operative efforts of scholarship, which have led to the UNESCO-sponsored *History of the Scientific and Cultural Development of Mankind*, are symptomatic of this trend.

To some extent the process of education is an opportunity for conserving, transmitting and renewing culture. Obviously, the approach to the teaching of history is an important part of this process. The kind of "rootedness" in time that children will have achieved when they leave school will have a potent influence on their relationship to their present and their future.

1

In order to build a positive future there is an urgent need for many individuals to be the possessors of a rich and imaginative historical perspective. A wholesome grasp of the processes of history can help us to retain and develop the best elements in Western civilization while giving proper weight to other cultures.

The culture of Western thought and science has been centrally developed in Europe for centuries and the United States of America has had a unique relationship to it. One might well consider the U.S.A. a testing ground for Western civilization. As the heir to the heritage of old Europe, whose populations have been combined to create him, *Homo Americanus* is something new on the earth. As the U.S.A. is one of the world's great powers, it is vital not only for him but for all mankind that he should develop a true picture of what a human being is. Whether he comes to think of himself as a little lower than the angels or a little higher than the monkeys is a responsibility, at least in some measure, of his schools and their history programs.

The subject matter of history defies limits. No mind can encompass it. Should the teacher begin in the dim twilight of prehistory? It is questionable whether he, let alone his pupils, has the imaginative ability to experience what a time span of two and a half million years signifies. Two and a half million years is the estimate for the Pleistocene Ice Age provided by the *Times Atlas of World History*. If we want children to *experience* process in history, we will not begin with such abstract conclusions. Rather will we ask: Are there key experiences in history that are as essential as the alphabet is for the formation of words? A mere handful of sounds leads to a universe of words. Are there equally fundamental historical elements that have to be brought to a child before he can become competent and free to assess historical processes himself? Rudolf Steiner, the founder of Waldorf education, considered this question in its relationship to another. Is there, he asked, an inner correlation between the development of a child's faculties and his approach to history? Can the methods of presentation, of historical involvement, be so improved that the pupil will later develop a truly healthy sense for history?

In order to treat these questions in a practical way that throws light on the Waldorf curriculum, let us first make a qualitative distinction between two kinds of historical experience. The contrasting attitude of two notable Americans, John Gunther and George Washington Carver, can illustrate the difference. Both attitudes and modes of experience play their positive role in childhood.

John Gunther seems to possess an unquenchable thirst for accurate knowledge of human affairs. His appetite for facts is equalled only by his industry. He tells us that it required more than forty thousand miles of travel to complete the research for his book *Inside Africa*, during which he meticulously recorded the answers to a steady flow of questions. These questions were no respecters of mealtimes. During one five-week period, for example, he had only one meal, breakfast excluded, that was not an interview. When the trip was over he had notes on one thousand five hundred and three conversations. No wonder that he writes, ''My real bibliography is people . . . In general, but not always in detail, the structure of this book follows the chronology of our trip.''

Gunther presents a surface conspectus of man in relation to a continent. He reveals facts as he assimilated and sifted them. But we never forget that these are part of his own journey. As he moves from one event to the next, he skillfully and swiftly assesses the immediate interaction of the materials he has gathered. The ''Inside'' books rightly claim breadth rather than depth. One might call them *horizontal studies* of culture. Each book covers a wide area with a factual mosaic. But the subject matter, be it an interview of a political nature of the description of a landscape, is always a picture containing the author. Gunther observing, Gunther recording, Gunther savoring the unfamiliar detail like a wine connoisseur who enjoys a rare vintage, is an essential part of this kind of presentation.

George Washington Carver died on June 5, 1943. This great agricultural scientist combined extraordinary creative gifts with a humility and richness of humanity that make his biography a truly inspiring document. Theodore Roosevelt spoke of him as ''not a man only, but a life transfused with passion for the enlarging and enriching of the lives of his fellow men.'' The harmonious fusion of life and

work achieved by Dr. Carver was brought about consciously and methodically. Sometimes he would describe
his approach to his students in words like these:

"I say 'tree' to you. The tree being one of several thousand members of the vegetable kingdom! You have no idea
what I mean! You are more confused than before I spoke
the word. The extent is too great. I say, 'oak tree', and
immediately thousands are shut out. You are now getting
information! Before, the word was just a generality.

"But you still don't know what I mean. Why call it
'oak'? It has certain qualities! It belongs to the genus
Quercus and contains the glucoside quercitrin. All oaks
contain that, and you can split it up and have stains and
dyes. Now you are beginning to get somewhere; you have
more information.

"But the extent is still too large. I narrow to 'white oak'.
There are a hundred or more varieties of oak, but we are
now down to two; there are only two white oaks. What is
the difference? They grow in different localities—one
upland and one bottom. The upland is exceedingly tough
and makes the best vehicles because of its unusual strength
and elasticity. In the bottom, the cells are large, loose and
open, because they must take in plenty of water. The wood
is black and fairly tears up in ribbons for making wicker-
work and baskets. All this time we have been getting more
information by decreasing the extent and increasing the
intent."

*Increasing the intent* might be taken as a motto for the

work of the man who cultivated the sweet potato, and for years meditated on the peanut, or "mani," as this plant was called by the Quechu. Carver did not find its value at once. In order to enrich arid and depleted soil, Professor Carver experimented with pod-bearing plants such as vetch, peas, beans, cloves and peanuts. All these belong to the Leguminosae family. This plant group has the special ability to extract nitrogen from the air and impart it to the soil. The roots have little swellings, "nodules," as they are called, the cells of which contain bacteria that can fix air nitrogen and make it available as plant food. When such roots decay, nitrogen is released in the soil for other hungry plants. Four hundred and twenty genera with several thousand species make up this vast family of seed plants. Carver worked patiently. Eventually he came to a decision in favor of the peanut. Easy to plant, easy to grow, easy to harvest, the peanut was already well-known to the Incas. They buried peanuts with their dead. The plant made its way to Africa in the seventeenth century. Later it was used by the slave traders as a food for their captives. In this way it returned to America.

Carver found that pound for pound the peanut topped sirloin for proteins, the best potatoes for carbohydrates and the best butter for fat. He invented innumerable uses for the plant he reintroduced to rescue the South from cotton disease and the dangers of an arid soil. He produced a highly effective medicinal oil, thirty different dyes, milk, cereal coffee—indeed, testifying before a congressional committee, he elaborated one hundred and seven products.

He was a selfless and indefatigable worker; always ready to be helpful; never using his unique abilities for economic gain. One might have encountered Carver early in the morning amid the trees. There, meditating in the laboratory of nature, he delved beneath the surface of the essences of nature. The mood of these early morning walks was not so different from the mood of the lines by Tennyson, which he so much loved when he was a boy:

> I hold you here, root and all, in my hand,
> Little flower—but if I could understand
> What you are, root and all, and all in all
> I would know what God and man is.

He continued to love those lines in his old age. For him, the world was full of layers of meaning. Each of God's plants contained untold depths. Carver worked on his own consciousness to plumb those depths.

To the historian, modern man has also to be studied depthwise. He has within him the achievement of vast civilizations. He is the result of the past. A study of the phases of consciousness through which mankind has passed can make us aware of unconscious layers in ourselves, of essences in our being that can become creative and productive. Any given moment of history is the past hurtling through the present into the future. When we experience this, the human soul is in the position of the sleeping princess in the fairy tale. Prince History awakens her to a different kind of life. She becomes aware of portions of her nature that transform her into an adult queen.

Gunther's methods are those of a historian concerned with the extent of history—which is global. Carver can help us to find the intent of history—ourselves. Through a living picture of man's development we discover where we stand.

Here we confront a dual task of history-teaching, which, in the curriculum of a Waldorf school, is separated. The extensive surface approach begins earlier than the focus on the changing consciousness of men as expressed in the cultures of the past. For the latter, the Waldorf teacher often reserves the name of "history." The "extensive" treatment is usually linked to the teaching of geography. A brief examination of the general structure of the geography curriculum is consequently a necessary prelude to our discussion of the history curriculum proper. One might ask whether this is an artificial separation. But the degree of mental maturity required for the study of civilizations is different from that called upon when studies are oriented toward a surface exploration of history that takes its beginning from life as we find it today.

# II

# History and Geography

The word *Geography* was probably coined by Eratosthenes of Alexandria who was the first to calculate the circumference of the earth. The three hundred years preceding his discovery had given Greek geography its characteristic stamp. Thales, the first of the Milesian philosophers, devised a method of determining the position of ships at sea based on his knowledge of geometry, a skill he had acquired on a business trip to Egypt. Thus at the very beginning of Western geographical study, geometry and geography are intertwined.

Another central trait, evident in the early writings of geographers, is their preoccupation with map making. While Anaximander was the first to make a map of the world, local map making almost certainly started earlier and developed rapidly into a science. By the time Strabo wrote his geographical treatise (approximately 10 B.C.), a picture of the earth had emerged that is still familiar to us today. Strabo described a sphere with poles, equator, ecliptic, tropics, meridians of longitude and parallels of latitude. He too stressed the geometrical character of his work. He warned the reader that in order to understand his treatise he would need a good grounding in geometry. Referring to the "lazy reader" he wrote, "If he does not know what a straight line is, or a curve, or a circle, or the difference between a spherical or a plane surface, then he must first acquaint himself with studies preparatory to a knowledge of geography." It is interesting that the geography curriculum, as outlined by Rudolf Steiner, commences where our geographic concepts historically also commenced; namely, with map making and with problems of spatial orientation. "Geography," he said in a lecture to teachers, "we can support through natural history, through geometry, as we draw maps in which we insert concepts of physical geography—we take geography through all these, and finally relate it to history."

It is in the fourth grade that the first geography main lesson takes place. "Main Lesson" is the name given to a period of study that takes place at the beginning of each day for two hours. It is devoted to one subject for three, four, or even five weeks at a time. This first geography main lesson period, or block as it is sometimes called, deals with the local environment and is centered in the child himself. Just as a stone dropping into a pool makes ever-widening eddies, so the teacher, perhaps commencing in the very classroom in which the lesson takes place, awakens the spatial awareness of his pupil and helps him to become conscious of ever-widening circles in his surroundings. How did he come to school? How does he move from his desk to the door? What path has to be followed from the classroom to the craft room? How is the school related to other houses in the same block? How is the block related to the rest of the district? And, how does the district fit into the town, the town into the county, the county into the state . . . ? Here are themes for maps. The initial drawings are based on immediate experience; later maps show rivers, mountains, the distribution of vegetation as well as transportation routes.

Starting with the position of the child means that the commencement of geography teaching will vary from Waldorf to Waldorf school, depending on its location. If the school is located in California, for example, the variety of natural phenomena; the contrast of climatic conditions, the profound influence of water—or the lack of water—on the lives of the people; the interrelation of nature and industry form intriguing themes all of which open doors into the past.

In the North we find sparkling lakes and swift mountain torrents that carve deep, rocky canyons. The lakes reflect the rugged Sierras thickly clad with forests of evergreen on the lower slopes. Nature has made this the home of lumberman and rancher—the paradise of angler, hunter and skier. For here snow falls often, early and late, sometimes piling twenty feet deep. Life under such conditions can be profitably contrasted with the rhythm of existence in Central Valley, one of the world's most productive areas. This valley is completely walled in by mountains. There is only one gap at San Francisco. The children should learn how water has given life to the valley. Starting with the once fiery volcano, Mt. Shasta, the children might study what happens to the Sacramento River at Shasta Dam. Here they can observe natural forces modified by human consciousness. Canals and pumps regulate the water on its journey to the parched but fertile acres of the southlands. The result is a life among orchards. From the same Central Valley come almost all our lemons, almonds, avocados, walnuts, olives, dates, grapes, figs and apricots. Imperial Valley, of course, is equally dependent on the Colorado River via the All-American Canal.

The Franciscan missions; gold; the sixty kinds of commercial minerals mined and processed in the State; the extensive fisheries and dock yards; the characteristics of the deserts; all these themes, and many others, can also reveal something of the area's history.

In this manner we describe to the child something of the interrelationship between geography and economic conditions. We do not necessarily continue to study areas side by side. After California the teacher might go quite far afield—even to other continents.

When grades seven and eight are reached, the emphasis shifts to cultural questions, for geographical factors also modify the culture of a people. The mentality of human beings living under sparse conditions in the cold is quite different from that of men situated in the midst of the prolific growth of the equator. Culture can be affected by lack of space—as in Japan . . . Dramatically colorful and rugged areas, very thinly populated, as in Norway, can be an equally profound influence on the mentality of a people . . . There is no doubt that the culture of Britain would have been quite different if the country were not an island . . . With but a little thought, any teacher of geography can find many other such examples. The study of the interrelation of natural factors with spiritual life, however, is a matter of greater subtlety than the study of economic geography with its historical ramifications.

How geographical conditions can affect the spiritual outlook of individuals and groups requires a sense of proportion and a degree of maturity we can expect in a child attending grade seven or eight, but hardly before.

Rudolf Steiner also indicated that it would be of value in the high school to spend some time on questions in which geography and law overlap. At present there are, for example, interesting discussions about global pollution problems. The issues involved are important and quite complicated. They can prove quite stimulating for an adolescent who can test his thought processes on real issues of the day. Through the study of an inventive genius like Jacques-Yves Cousteau, who in the late 60's realized that the unbridled technological developments of the present threaten the oceans and the water resources of our planet, they can reflect on the battle between noble thought and the greed that is rarely far away from questions of international law. Cousteau's *Basic Principles for a Global Ocean Policy* and his *A Bill of Rights for Future Generations* are short enough to form a suitable basis for prepared discussions. Such problems of international law, however, insofar as they relate to geographic factors, also have important if little known historical aspects that need to be researched.

So, by way of summary, we might speak of three areas in which the teaching of geography and the teaching of history overlap. In grades four, five and six the Waldorf teacher emphasizes the area of production. The pupil learns how all man's goods are gifts of earth. This can also help him to acquire a sense of responsibility for the planet as a whole. In grades seven and eight the teacher focuses on the meeting of man and nature with a cultural, rather than economic, emphasis. In the high school he seeks out opportunities to show how man has ordered his steward-ship of the earth with the help of law.

Any historical knowledge gained in this process might be classified as "things modern people ought to know." In other words, qualitatively, it belongs to the approach that we have previously characterized as the extensive horizontal approach.

# III

## The History of Civilizations

The fundamental concept behind our teaching of history is that the individual is an end in himself, not an instrument to be used by others in the pursuit of some ulterior purpose.

The barbarian is not yet an individual, and he has no history. He neither invents nor progresses, but like an animal he lives at the mercy of his environment. He takes his first step in the direction of civilization when he acquires the desire to change, and begins to invent. The civilized man, like all men, is born weak and helpless, but because he lives within a changing environment, the work of his predecessors, the possibilities for improvement are limitless, and the notion of progress is always before him.

The great civilizations of the past are all different. Each one gives us an opportunity to enter imaginatively into a world dissimilar to our own. We can turn to Assyria, Babylonia, Egypt, the birth of China, or Mohenjo-daro and the Indus civilization, and in each case discern a unique character permeating the whole culture and coming to expression in its parts as well. This "character" can be compared to the way individual character comes to expression in the life of a person.

When we concern ourselves with the biography of a great artist we repeatedly confront a polarity. We inevitably find much that he has in common with his contemporaries. On the most obvious level there is his body, each part of which is overwhelmingly similar to that of his fellow men. Yet, his physique and his gestures also will be subtly characteristic of his identity. The artist will share in the customs and traditional modes of expression of his time, and yet both the pattern of his speech and his handwriting can always be identified as peculiarly his own. At times the technique he uses will be so permeated with his being that a mere fragment of a painting is enough to evoke recognition of his specific contribution.

The author of *Kingship and the Gods*, Henri Frankfort, reflecting on this theme in *The Intellectual Adventure of Ancient Man*, called the vital identity of a civilization its *form*. He looked for the "form" in a certain coherence among its various manifestations, a certain consistency in its orientation, a certain cultural style that shaped its judicial and political institutions, its art as well as its literature, its religion as well as its morals. Frankfort sees the emergence of this "form" not as a slow evolution but as the outcome of a sudden and intense change producing a rapid maturity. This first bloom of a new cultural impulse is usually followed by a long period of internal development more or less affected by outside influences.

But the concept of development must not be confused with the idea of progress as advocated by the French Enlightenment and by many writers of the nineteenth century. When Voltaire's contemporary, the Marquis de

Condorcet, wrote his *Sketch of an Historical Picture of the Human Mind*, he elaborated ten phases of history, each a linear improvement on the one before it, for the explicit purpose of establishing the idea of irreversible progress. Condorcet was convinced that this straight line evolution was guaranteed by the scientific enlightenment that could only bring about the constant improvement of social conditions. In the nineteenth century the idea of progress received further reinforcement from directions as different as the thought structure of Darwinian evolutionary theory and Marxian materialism.

Even J. H. Newman wrote: "Civilization is that state to which man's nature points and tends; it is the systematic use, improvement, and combination of those faculties which are his characteristic; and viewed in its idea, it is the perfection, the happiness of our mortal state."

If this were wholly true we should expect to perceive an ascending line of progress in the history of mankind, and each phase of civilization would be "more perfect" than the preceding one.

But this is precisely what we do *not* see in history. What we see is the growth and decline of separate civilizations, not one ascending line of "civilization." It cannot be demonstrated—popular belief to the contrary—that present-day man is an improvement in all respects over men of earlier times because of his superior rational mind. It is therefore more helpful to use the concept of culture rather than that of civilization, since most of us are ready to allow some merit to earlier cultures. Culture suggests the complex of attainments, beliefs, customs, traditions and the like, which form the background of a particular people or group, distinguishing them from all other peoples or groups, and giving their particular civilization, no matter how little or how far advanced, its peculiar quality or character.

One of the most stimulating aspects of history is a study of the qualitative differences of various cultures. This kind of history reveals that man undergoes a development of consciousness. Not that in any quantitative sense he has ''more'' or ''less'' consciousness at any given moment of time, but that he unfolds different nuances of his soul in different epochs. Even in the span of an individual life we cannot speak of the totality of a person coming to full expression at any given moment of time. In order to assess an individual, we require his full biography. Such a biography often varies greatly, and most unexpectedly, from one time of life to another. So it is with history. The biography of Man comes to expression in the manifoldness of people and cultures, in a great variety of world conceptions, and in changing attitudes to life.

One of the first points essential to the understanding of any ancient culture is that men had an entirely different attitude toward any kind of observed process. When we immerse ourselves in antiquity we immediately encounter something foreign to our age—a myth-making mentality. Thus, while the modern visitor can well echo Herodotus's observation that Egypt is the gift of the Nile, he finds that it is difficult to attune himself to the ancient Egyptians who made the River the very center of their religious thought.

Already in the dim twilight of prehistory, the Nile had been worshipped in the guise of the god Hapi, a male deity with great hanging female breasts from which gushed life-giving water. The figure was usually depicted as sitting in the shallows of his river and holding over his head a sheaf of lotus plants, their pads and bright blue flowers showing on the surface of the water. Ancient Egyptians held the land had had its genesis from the primeval male-female waters, which had shrunk back into a vast circling flood around the earth. Only the Nile still flowed out from this life-creating stream. But only a portion of it crossed the desert, for one part of the Nile became a river in the sky, crossing the world of light and thick darkness. The Egyptian looked up to the Milky Way and saw the luminous river that, during the day, carried the boat of his sun god, Ra. As Egypt developed from predynastic times to its complex fulfillment as a civilization, many other gods were worshipped, but Hapi and Ra, water and sunlight, remained at the center of Egyptian religious belief.

We must not think of "religious belief" as a conceptual category apart—for the Egyptian of the Old Kingdom had no other. Science and art had an applied purpose, and that purpose was indissolubly related to religion. As John Wilson writes in his *Culture of Ancient Egypt*, "All phases of life carried a strong coloration of the sacred, from the beginning down to the first important secularization under the empire.'' In other words, from approximately 2700 B.C. to 1465 B.C., every aspect of the Egyptian system of life was centered in religion. The key factor of this system was the view that the land of Egypt and the ruler of Egypt were one being and had one identity. The Pharaoh was the State, and of course he was a god.

Today, we cannot make any sense of such concepts, and consequently cannot understand the ancient Egyptians unless we make the effort to examine some of their other basic ideas. They held that the gods had provided the model for the human body, this model being a spiritual organism endowed with life and many interweaving forces of a non-physical nature. The sun god Ra ordered that man was to receive this invisible entity, which the priests often likened to a figure of light at birth. This gift of Ra was called ''Ka.'' Ka is life itself. Man lives while ''he is master of his Ka,'' or while ''he goes with his Ka.'' Hieroglyphics teach us that the Ka is a kind of double; children have small Ka's, grown-ups, larger ones. The physical form and the invisible Ka that governs growth, nourishment and reproduction, correspond and cover each other. An old myth reveals that the human Ka is born out of the Ka's of the sun god Ra—the possessor of fourteen Ka's. The light organism, Ka, born out of the sun's spirit, becomes the intermediary between the afterlife world and the period spent in Egypt. Moreover, in man the Ka finds his reflection, for it is not man who nourishes himself, but the life forces of the sun that nourish him.

The Pharaoh was not revered as a personality, but as the bearer of the most complete Ka. His whole being was permeated with "righteousness." It is this Ka of the Pharaoh that received the "Horus name" when he ascended the throne. Osiris, judge of the soul in the afterlife, only created Horus after his own death. Horus, who changes the headdress of Isis, transforming past into future, is chiefly active in the world of spirit. The Ka also fulfills its mission in the afterlife. Here, perhaps, we come to the most fundamental trait in Egyptian civilization, the concern with the afterlife.

It is not for the historian to judge in how far the Pharaoh, who was also the chief high priest, was in reality the most highly evolved of his people. It *is* for him to show how the yardstick of everyday existence at all social levels was the current view of the afterlife. This view lies embedded in mighty imaginations, particularly in the body of legend and myth surrounding the figure Thoth-Hermes, who accompanies the dead to the Osiris judgment of the soul. Nothing can be more historically concrete than the mythology of the ancient Egyptians—it is hewn in stones, protected to the best of their abilities in temples and pyramids.

When the teacher tries to acquaint himself with the manifoldness of Egyptian beliefs, he discovers many unre-

lated and contradictory explanations accepted side by
side. Formidable difficulties are presented by the accumu-
lation of Egyptian thought over the centuries. Men seemed
reluctant to replace an established idea with a new one, or
to discard images of older times. Two gods were frequently
assimilated with one another without losing their separate
entities. The history teacher may well come to the conclusion that the Egyptian experience of divinity was a
phenomenon approached from many viewpoints, for religious experience was in no way theoretical. It was as real as
a sense impression is to us. Just as we can approach a
mountain top from different slopes, so they approached
their peaks of reality from many sides.

It is the manifold nature of Egyptian religious tradition
and belief that defies summary treatment. All the same, it
is a valuable experience for teacher and children to live,
for a short spell, in a mental climate that lacks the hard
contours of logic. The background of mythology with all
its mysterious lights and shadows is necessary for an
understanding of Egypt's clearer message—its architecture, its sculpture and the details of everyday life that
have accumulated in growing profusion ever since Napoleon's march into Egypt in the year 1798.

There are many stimulating and profitable themes for
one who is seeking a picture of the totality of Egyptian
life. The study of such themes is useful as a preparatory
activity for the teacher. We shall see later that, in a Waldorf school, the technique of teaching history at this age

level makes yet quite other demands on the teacher. While he himself must have a clear conception of the development of at least some of these themes, he cannot use his knowledge directly.

The temptation to discuss the relative merits of materials available is great, but within the scope of this short study, all we have room for is a telegraphic mention of a series of paths of discovery, each of which yields valuable images.

The themes listed here are nothing more than fingers pointing to some of those springs that quicken the historical imagination: Life in the temples; Heliopolis and the creation myth of Atum-Ra; the central myth of Egyptian religion and of the state, the story of Isis, Osiris and Horus; Menes, the creation of Memphis and the transcendent deity Ptah; Pharaoh Djoser and his famous helper Imhotep in the midst of the wonderful group of temples and courts surrounding the Step Pyramid of Sakkara; Menthuhotep and Thebes at the beginning of the middle kingdom; the monist, Akhenaten, his newly created holy city of El-Amarna, and his short-lived cultural revolution; Rameses II, father of more than 150 sons and daughters, successful general, extravagant builder of the titanic hypostyle hall at Karnak, the Rameseum in western Thebes and the rock-cut Nubian temples of Abu Simbel; irrigation, agriculture and animal husbandry; the Sothis periods and the rotating festivals of the year; trade, commerce and the impact of limited communication with other peoples . . . the story of Egyptian writing . . . and, most fundamental of all, the Egyptian attitudes toward death.

Ideally, the teacher should not rest until the fusion of such materials within himself enables him to describe in graphic detail the life of an ordinary Egyptian from dawn to dusk— and into the night. How did a stonemason at Giza do his arithmetic? How did he eat? What did he know? What did he believe? How was he related to the rest of Egyptian society? Just as a piece of poetry is made up of metrical variations against a basic meter that forms the body of the poem, so also successful history teaching is dependent on such basic background materials. The figures placed in the foreground by the history teacher breathe and inspire only when they are correctly related to the tones weaving around them as the background of their time.

From the point of view of a schedule the whole of such an Egyptian experience may well have to be concentrated into one week of main lessons.

In many ways Mesopotamia can be contrasted with Egypt. Two rivers run through the length of its plain. But the Tigris is of little use for irrigation purposes because of its deeply cut bed. The normal water level lies too low beneath that of the surrounding country for the river to be tapped by any simple canal system. This leaves the Euphrates as a water source for agriculture. The contrast between the Nile and the Euphrates is instructive. The Euphrates carries loam and lime in its swift currents. When the river flows into the flat alluvium of the delta, much sediment is deposited. The river bed is raised thereby and high banks are formed on either side. In this way the whole river runs above the level of the plain and can easily be diverted for the benefit of the fields alongside.

A constant task was to maintain and strengthen the banks of the Euphrates so that crops would not be submerged at the wrong time. The major difficulty was not irrigation but drainage as superfluous water was prone to create pools and stagnant swamps. The Nile flooded at predictable times; the Euphrates was more erratic. It flooded when the far away snows of the mountainous regions of the Anatolia melted, and this happened between the beginning of April and early June. Thus in Egypt, Hapi, the god of inundation, was a beneficent diety; in Mesopotamia, Nin-Girsu and Tiamet were regarded as malevolent powers that had to be over-come. The control of the water demanded much labor and elaborate organization.

The earliest fully historical phase in Mesopotamia begins close to 2800 B.C. and ends with the accession of the first great empire builder, Sargon of Akhud in 2340 B.C. But the division between history and prehistory is more arbitrary than in Egypt because there is no secure anchor time for dating. Furthermore, Sumarian cities ruled over by ensis, assemblies consisting of adult free males and a body of aristocratic elders, were already flourishing before 2800. Indeed, the leading city of Uruk already had a *lugal*, or king. The concept and function of the lugal changed much more than that of the Pharaoh, but from the beginning it was characteristically different.

The prehistoric mythology of the valley of the twin rivers from the time when the form of the Sumarian civilization was first emerging is lost to us. Much of it, however, has come down to us in later, probably largely accurate, versions of the *Enuma Elish*, the Babylonian creation myth. The stories of the Enuma Elish embody a vision of the cosmos and its governance. Some historians assume that this divine state was a projection of the order prevailing on earth, but it would be more in harmony with the stage of consciousness of those times to hypothesize that the organization of society was modelled on the view of cosmic organization.

In the pantheon of the gods the first course of authority was Anu, the lofty sky god. Enlil, god of storm, provided the force necessary for the will of authority to be imposed. Enlil could delegate this power to other divinities or to human beings. But neither Anu or Enlil were absolute authorities, they acted after consultation with a formal assembly of all the gods.

As Jacgnetta Hawks wrote in her book *The First Great Civilizations:* "Taken together, the testimony of records, epic and mythological stories leave no doubt that the Sumarian city-states emerged into history with a dual assembling of elders and citizens. The appointed lugal in his changing role was priestly lord, governor, and king.

All Sumarian rulers originally had their residence within
the temple precincts. In early dynastic times, however,
the growing power of the throne had already brought
about a division between religious leadership and secular
rule. For many centuries the city-states of Sumer and
Akhud were dominated by the dual authority of temple
and palace, with the palace growing in power. The "king's
house" became the apex of a separate secular and military hierarchy with its fields and client farmers, its arti-
sans and many slaves, its scribes and its soldiers."

In contradistinction to the Egyptians, the gateway of
science for the Babylonians was algebra and not arithmetic. In Egypt the priests moved from practical calcula-
tions, which were largely simple addition, to a decimal
system. Egyptian arithmetic became the basis of a geometry that was applied by the water administration and that
achieved its most elaborate refinement in the proportions
and structure of the pyramid. As far as we know from the
Rind Papyrus, our main source of information, they
never formulated general principles in writing. We have
quite a number of Babylonian algebraic texts, and these
set out problems but do not provide general formulae.
Both Egypt and Babylon shunned abstractions. Yet Babylonian mathematics had an elaborate thought structure
implicit in it. Already the Sumerians, their predecessors,
had invented a sexagesimal notation for whole numbers
and for fractions as well as a sexagesimal system of

weights and measures. They developed a sophisticated notation in which the position of notation was necessary for the algebra and astronomy of the Babylonians.

While the Egyptian calendar was based on the annual flooding of the Nile, which recurred with reasonable regularity, the Mesopotamian calendar was astronomically based. The moon god, Nannar, ruled time. The calendar contained twelve lunar months of twenty-nine or thirty days. The resulting irregularities became confusing because the months were given different names in different city-states. The nomenclature and the rhythm of festival days was only stabilized in Hammurabi's Babylonia, that is, in approximately 1763 B.C.

The mathematical achievements of Babylonian astronomy are remarkable and much superior to those of the Egyptians. They knew much about the duration of day and night in different seasons of the year, the rising and setting of the moon, and the appearance and disappearance of Venus. From the time of the third dynasty of Ur, approximately 2100 B.C., we have many "omen tablets." These texts combine astrological forecasts with astronomical observations. Astrology was fully integrated into astronomy, and the star-script was seen as the language of the gods.

One attraction of the Assyro-Babylonian world for the Waldorf teacher is the heritage of literature, which carried the distinct flavor of Mesopotamian spiritual life into Asia Minor, Syria, Persia and Egypt. It is a flavor that still communicates the form of this civilization to the twentieth century child when the stories are carefully absorbed and freely retold.

This literature, which was initially part of an oral temple tradition, was faithfully preserved by the scribes of the Sumerian *eddubas*. The scholars of the eddubas, and of the schools that came later, remained marvelously faithful to tradition. Their reverence kept alive a deceased language and a prehistoric mythology. Their humanity recorded delightfully humorous proverbs, interesting secular prose, and some historical narratives, as well as great myths and epics.

Probably the two most influential works were *The Seven Tablets of Creation* and the epic of *Gilgamesh*.

*The Seven Tablets of Creation*, or *Enumah Elish*, as it is also called, is clearly rendered into English with valuable notes in *Voices From The Clay* by Silvestro Fiore. In the later periods of Babylonian civilization this composition was always recited on the fourth day of the New Year Festival. The hero of the poem is Marduk, who continues the creation of the gods and gains kingship over the universe in the process.

*The Epic of Gilgamesh* is undoubtedly the finest work of Babylonian literature available to us. It was always popular and many versions have been found. It was translated into Hurran and Hittite. Neo-Assyrian and Akkudian versions render the story with variations. The most complete account was found in Nineveh. The poem consists of twelve tablets, each tablet corresponding to a zodiacal station. Gilgamesh, a legendary king of Uruk, for whom there is a historical basis, and his wild-man companion, Enkidu, enact events on earth that reflect cosmic processes. Rudolf Steiner makes a stimulating contribution to the understanding of the place of the Gilgamesh epic in the history of consciousness in two lecture cycles delivered eleven years apart. The first was given in Stuttgart, Germany from December 27, 1910; the second in Dornach, Switzerland from December 24, 1923 to January 1, 1924.

Another important poem, probably one of the oldest myths in Mesopotamia, is *Ishtar's Descent to the Netherworld.* This great myth is, unfortunately, not always available in an accurate rendition. It is contained in the L. W. King collection, *Cuneiform Texts From Babylonian Tablets in the British Museum.* Among later more secular compositions popular works like *The Poor Man of Nippur* and *The Pessimistic Dialogue Between Master and Servant* deserve attention.

As defined by urban life and writing, civilization began in Mesopotamia and Egypt and soon spread to Elam, the Indus Valley, Crete and Asia Minor.

Not every Waldorf teacher will begin with these civilizations. Some will devote the beginning of their ancient history period to an excursus into prehistory. They might delve into times in India and Persia where evidence of mythology and archeology, though limited, is interesting because it demonstrates that human beings alive in those prehistoric times had quite other modes of consciousness. Then again, the class teacher might well include India at the time of the Rig-Veda. In an age when much is made of the class concept, a knowledge of how the Indian caste system evolved can be valuable for life. It can lead to an understanding of attitudes toward the class question in earlier times, which is essential if the children are ever to understand the East of the past and of the present.

The Indian word for caste is "Varna," which actually means color. There are three main characteristics of caste: *heredity*—caste cannot be changed; *endogamy*—marriage must take place within the caste and no member can marry outside it; *restrictions*—there are regulations regarding the acceptance of food and drink from members of other castes. Under the Gupta kings (330 to 450 A.D.) this system hardened into such a rigid form that it has remained a problem to this day. There were two earlier phases when the system was not so inflexible. In Buddhist times (600 to 300 B.C.) the cardinal factor was not birth but the spiritual evolution of a man. There were no marriage restrictions. According to one account, Buddha himself married outside his caste.

If we go back still further to the period of the Vedas (1500 to 600 B.C.), we find that instead of the many castes we have four classes only: the Brahmins; the Ksatriyas (warriors); the Vaisyas (craftsmen and agriculturists); the Sudras (menials).

The great scholar-president of India, Radhakrishnan,

in his book *Eastern Religions and Western Thought* points out that the earliest reference to these four classes is in the Purusa Sukta of the Rig-Veda, where they are described as having sprung from the body of the creative spirit—from his head, arms, thighs and feet. This poetical image is intended to convey the organic character of society. "Human society is an attempt to express in social life the cosmic purpose, which has other ways of expression in the material and the supramaterial planes."

Radhakrishnan goes on to characterize the Brahmins as the priest class whose function it is to seek and find knowledge. The true Brahmin is said to be one who has sensed the deepest self and acts out of that consciousness. Immediate needs, practical administration, power in any form, are not for him. Radhakrishnan argues that today we also need such a group, selected, not on a racial basis, but on the grounds of inner stature. "Those who belong to the spiritual ministry of society," he writes, "must guard their integrity of mind as a sacred possession, be completely masters of themselves, and proclaim the truth that all cities, all states, all kingdoms, are mortal, and only the spirit of man immortal."

Ksatriyas are the practical administrators, the politicians, and the warriors. Their qualities are as necessary to the body social as the enlightenment of the Brahmins. The Vaisyas are equally necessary and appreciated. Unfortunately, the Sudras, the workers, were given a lower evaluation in India. Probably this was due to the fact that they were descendants of the aboriginal population, while the other three groups belonged to the Aryan conquerors. In addition to these there are also mixed castes. In southern India these have been named pariahs. The lowest of all the mixed castes are the Candalas who are descended from the Brahmins on the mother's side and from Sudras on the father's.

There is an essential difference between the concept of class held by the early Indians and the later idea of caste. In the class order of the Purusa Sukta anyone who had the courage to undergo the discipline, the strength to deny himself the pleasures of life, and the capacity to develop his faculties was free in theory to join any class. In practice, the advantages of race, environment and opportunity were so great that they were usually decisive. But the caste scheme does not allow for the free play of creative energies, nor does it rest on moral stature.

Yet, even after the caste system had become a fossil of a onetime reality, men accepted it without a murmur. It is hard for the children to understand this when they hear the description of a Brahmin followed by that of an outcast. Why should a Candalas accept the treatment he receives? In the background of this acceptance of caste stands the Indian concern with the laws of reincarnation and karma. It is generally believed that as the individual passed from life to life, he also passed from caste to caste according to his moral record. Only when, through intensive self development, an individual passed beyond the bounds of his karma, did he move from one caste to another during the span of one lifetime. Here again, one can see how the general tapestry of religious belief was decisive in the pattern of everyday living.

Whether or not India is dealt with in grade five, and there are many powerful arguments in its favor, the major contrast should be made between Egypt and Greece. This permits the use of some Indian material in connection with the campaigns of Alexander the Great, who was the first Western leader to make contact with Indian civilization.

The geographical contrast between Egypt and Greece makes a dramatic introduction to the study of Greece in the classroom. Without the Nile, the land of Egypt would wither to dust and be blown away. There would be nothing but a vast dry wadi of the great North African Desert. With the Nile, and with the help of methodical irrigation, man has learned to battle with the encroaching sands. The Isles of Greece, on the other hand, throughout the ages have battled with the waves. The waters of the Mediterranean and the Aegean have plastically fashioned the land. Here the earth speaks through the mouth of the volcano. Here land was lifted from the ocean bed, and mountain ranges were covered with water in an active interplay of the earth's natural forces. No other country of similar size can boast such an astonishing length of coastline. The variety of convolutions is more than matched by the variety contained in the geologically young limestone ranges. The mountains are steep, rugged and grand. They are often intersected with rivers, difficult to cross.

In Ancient Greece, kingdoms could thrive side by side with little contact because of the natural barriers that caused great difficulties of communication—whereas in Egypt the desert sands presented no obstacle. In Greece, areas of stark bareness and some snowy peaks contrast with grasslands and forests, including pockets of great fertility. There is more of the sense of sameness in the desert.

The Egyptian regarded himself as in the center of the universe; the world extended to the rim of the desert. His empire was the world. The ancient Greeks found themselves, as Aristotle remarks, "in an intermediate position, halfway between the tropics and the cold lands of the north." Their knowledge, before the Hellenistic age, stopped absolutely at the Pillars of Hercules—the Rock of Gibraltar. In what was then regarded as the civilized world, the Aegean stands midway on all routes of trade and adventure. On the islands a many-colored quilt of races settled—prehistoric Achaeans, Aeolians, Ionians and Dorians. Turning northwards, there is clear evidence of intercourse between prehistoric Greece and Macedonia and the Danubian and Carpathian areas. Westward there are hints of relations with Italy, Sicily and Sardinia. In the Asia Minor direction, contact with Egypt, Palestine, Cyprus, and above all, Troy has been clearly established.

In this ferment of races, there was constant strife—

unlike the long, unbroken periods of peace in ancient Egypt.

A peculiar position in Greek mythology is held by the island of Crete. Four snowclad mountain groups, once heavily forested, which formerly linked the chains of the Pelopennesus with the mountains of southwestern Turkey, form a porous limestone arc that seems like a hundred-and-sixty-mile-long bridge from Egypt to Greece. Crete is more than a geographical link in a submerged chain. It is both the cradle of Hellas and a bridge to the understanding of the Greek mind. Here, according to tradition, we find the cave that is the birthplace of Zeus. Here, also, a mere three miles from Herakleion, we can delve back some four-thousand five-hundred years to the time of the ancient Minoans. To equal the grandeur of the palace of Minos at Knossos, we would have to travel to the heart of Egypt or Babylon.

Minos was powerful and needed no fortifications to protect him. Minoan ships ruled the sea, and foreign navies gave Crete a wide berth. This enabled him to live comfortably surrounded by beauty. There are still six-foot jars of Crete's best olive oil and remnants of beans, barley and other stores in his underground stockrooms. A beautiful fresco of the head of a sacred bull can remind us that the mighty palace of Knossos was also a religious center. This bull, so typical of Crete, requires an explanation that must lead us into the field of astronomy. In an astronomical sense, the entry into the Greek phase of human consciousness is marked by a transition from the Bull to the Ram.

The sun moves through the twelve zodiacal constellations displayed along the ecliptic in one year of 365¼ days. But it does not return exactly to the same point. This arresting of the sun short of the point that was reached the year before, is called the precession of the equinoxes. It makes the sun move westward opposite to the annual path, which moves eastward. So we can think of the sun, running through the twelve zodiacal constellations in one direction (eastward) in one year of 365¼ solar days, and in the opposite direction (westward) in 25,920 years. As a consequence, while the sun now rises in the beginning of spring in Pisces, at the time of Christ it rose in Aries. Legends and myths point to this supra-historical reality. The Egyptians worshipped the Apis Bull. Minos still had a Bull culture. Jason is already searching for the Golden Fleece of the Ram. Christ is considered as a Lamb bearing the sins of the world. These correspondences between myth, religious cults and astronomical events are an aid to historical study only when it is understood that the ancients did not regard the sun as entering into Aries until it had reached the midpoint of that sign.

Steiner called this 2160 year period during which the vernal point recedes through one sign of the zodiac a "cultural epoch." He often spoke of four such epochs

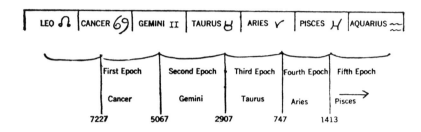

preceding our own age. These he named the Indian, Persian, Egyptian and Graeco-Roman Epochs.*

Such considerations are vital for an understanding of
the most essential story of Crete. This island was sub-
jected to Egyptian influences from the time of the conquest of Amenhopis the Third. So it is little wonder that
fundamentally Egyptian motifs are repeated at the court
of King Minos. Sculptures, as well as frescoes, show
stories of the sacred bull fights. The Homeric bards who
sang of "a dancing place bright gleaming" at Knossos,
bore this in mind. Here the mighty sea king Minos sacri-

---

*The teacher who includes scenes of Indian life in his grade five period
usually describes the civilization of the Vedic Aryans. The diagram makes it
clear that what Steiner has called the *Indian Epoch* in his writings antedates not
only the Vedic period but even the earlier civilizations based on Harappa and
Mohenjo-Daro.

Steiner has much to say on the first and second epochs that is most helpful for
an understanding of ancient mythology. But on the basis of present archaeological and literary research it is difficult, if not impossible, to cover these
epochs with any adequacy.

ficed Athenian youths and maidens to a man-eating bull kept in a maze. The myth further relates how the hostage, Theseus, killed the beast and escaped from the labyrinth by following the thread given him by Ariadne, the king's daughter.

Unlike earlier labyrinths, that of Crete was constructed by Daedalus, an engineer of Athenian descent. It was his joy to construct cosmic rhythms into machinery. For example, he invented a dance that imitated the movements of the stars. He instructed Ariadne in this dance and gave her the thread, also his invention, with the help of which she rescued Theseus. Following Ariadne's thread with his logical faculty, Theseus made his way through a representation of the windings of the human brain. It was this experience that enabled him at a later date to give Athens its social order and its festivals. We can therefore regard Theseus as the prototype of a new kind of human being, possessed of a soul configuration different from that of the past. He personifies the conquest of the rational mind over the legacy of antiquity.

The road to the discovery of self-consciousness was still a long one. The Dorians were inclined to subdue the individual to uniformity. The Aeolians revived the memories of the heroic age. Sparta unfolded the activity of the will. But it was the Ionian tribe that eventually achieved the greatest measure of harmony and universality of mind. In Athens constitutional innovations were a common occurrence, and ran the gamut from kingdom to oligarchy, from aristocracy to tyranny, and finally to democracy.

There are many preparatory steps to the wonder of Athens in the fifth century B. C. Through the cunning of Odysseus, Troy, the last outpost of matriarchy, had to fall. Here again, it is reason and intellect that characterize the Greeks. As Frederick Hiebel wrote in his *Gospel of Hellas:*

> After the Palladium had been carried away, Laocoon, the Priest of Troy, had to die with his two sons. His death represented the overcoming of sacerdotalism by the intellect. The myth describing the death of Laocoon and his sons emphasized the extinction of clairvoyance based on family ties on which the culture of Ilium was founded. The heroes of Troy were the sons of Priam; they were a clan. The Greeks, on the other hand, fought as personalities, each of them with his own mind, decision, mood and temper.
>
> Troy was at an end, Hellas was beginning. The path from Troy to Hellas led to the polis of the Greeks. The Trojan War signified the beginning of the dissolution of ancient blood ties. Paris, the son of Priam and a member of the royal clan, desired Helen of Argos to break away from the rule of blood ties on which the oriental consciousness was based.

It is perhaps noteworthy that the first Olympic Games, from which the Greeks date their calendar, were held in 776 B.C.—a few years before the beginning of the fourth cultural epoch (747 B.C.). The traditional date of the founding of Rome, closer still to this beginning date, was 753 B.C.

According to Kitto in *The Greeks*, we have Homer somewhere near mid-ninth century B.C. Through Hesiod a wealth of mythology permeated the eighth century B.C. In the seventh century we have the earliest of the Doric temples, that of Hera at Olympia. Early Doric temples, datable in the late seventh century, have also been discovered at Thermon, Korkyra (Corfu), Delphi and Cyrene. From that time on the incredibly beautiful architecture that culminated in the Parthenon and Acropolis of Athens in the fifth century developed with quantitative and qualitative momentum. The sixth century saw the birth of the self-governing polis under Solon, the threat of Darius and the Persian advance, the Peloponnesian League, and the birth of philosophy.

By the time the fifth century is reached, it would be good for the children of the fifth grade to move through the agora and the streets of Athens with more freedom than is possible in the streets of a modern city. Here they can meet a unique combination of knowledge, moderation and self-discipline. Here the human personality is given an absolute value against, if need be, the gods, the social group and the state. The very language has a remarkable tension between the concreteness of poetic imagery and the precision of abstract thought. As we pass through the polis, we can also observe a lively intellectual attempt to order and systematize the universe. The children should feel something of the enthusiasm that accompanied the first examination of the principles of geography, history, natural science, anatomy, medicine, psychology, grammar, prosody, politics, logic and philosophy. No somber caverns, no dark pyramids, but airy temples and statues proclaiming the glory of man—man in all his harmony—is the joyous overall impression they should be left with.

There was, of course, a darker side to life in Athens. The individual achievement of prominent Athenians rested on slavery. If we follow in the footsteps of Diocles, a well-to-do citizen, it becomes clear that such a man could not subsist on his own personal output of work!

He explains with care how to spend one's days hygienically. Arise before sunrise. Wash your face and hair, clean your teeth, massage your gums with powdered peppermint, and rub down the whole body with oil. Then take a short walk. In the course of the morning pay a visit to the gymnasium for bodily exercise. Follow these by a shower and by a massage. Breakfast comes late: a light meal, consisting of bread with a thin soup, some vegetables and perhaps a cucumber in season. If thirsty, drink water before the meal. Afterwards, a little white wine diluted with water and sweetened with honey is pleasant. This first meal is probably over a little after noon and, therefore, might well be followed with hours of siesta in a cool, shady, and retired spot. After rest, there is some time for the day's occupations, after which the gymnasium can again be visited. Finally, in the evening comes the chief meal, consisting of fruit, vegetables, bread, and fish or meat. Diocles further suggests a short walk might be taken before an early turn into bed.

From such accounts it is easy to see that the wondrous achievements of Greece were possible partly because many menial tasks were performed by slaves. Fortunately, we have balanced and detailed assessments of life in fifth-century Athens. Among these, Alfred Zimmern's *The Greek Commonwealth* makes the grocery bill and the home owners' problems particularly vivid. The children should experience the magnitude of the contribution of Athens; for unless our cultural standards are to be measured in terms of comfort and gadgetry, the Athens of this period was without a doubt the home of the most civilized society that has yet existed. For a brief spell, the Athenian also had a pervading sense of the common interest, a sense of unity, a spirit of wholeness as rare in the history of Greece as in that of more modern times.

The class five curriculum concludes with the times of Alexander the Great. In the subsequent year, Rome enters the classroom. Perhaps this is a good moment to make a pause and examine, not the background work of the teacher, but some of the techniques and methods he might use in a Waldorf school.

# IV

# Methods of Teaching

The American Historical Association in a published statement of the committee on teaching entitled, "Preparation of Secondary History School Teachers," pinpoints one of the major problems facing the practical educator in one terse sentence: "The harassed and overburdened history teacher needs reliable writings designed particularly with his needs in view." If this is true of specialists, what of Waldorf school class teachers who, in the course of eight years, have to introduce a great variety of subjects? They cannot be expected to be experts. They cannot know all the interweaving strands of influence, all the causes and effects of history. Indeed, it calls for a bold historian who will speak of an event being "caused" by an immediately preceding event. Challenge and response are no mechanical devices that can be calculated and appraised in the same manner that the movement of billiard balls can be worked out. How can the teacher save himself from misrepresentation due to lack of information? How, also, should he select? For his time necessitates limitation, and his knowledge might well travel along paths of inclination and consequently be biased. How?

This problem can be linked with a second, much more pernicious than the first, but not so often discussed. To

44

the Marxist there is a first law of history that is supposed to determine the direction of historical evolution. This law says that economic developments are basic to social evolution in other areas. Ideas and institutions, law and politics, even religious concepts and artistic expressions are part of the social "superstructure," inevitably changing with the gradual transformation of the economic foundation. The economic trend is primary, and all else are secondary phenomena. Individuality and free will are only regarded as conditioned reflexes of the economic process. The animal man has but one life force—economics. No one quite knows what Marx meant by his concept of economic change, but the assumption that he referred to a physical change basic to all social evolution is supported by a number of examples through which both he and Engels tried to elucidate their basic proposition. What Marx has not taken into account, and what we in Western education *must* take into account, is that economic processes, as well as all others, do not start in a vague sea of theoretical impulses, but in man himself. It was not a *process* that brought the steam engine into the world in a usable form—it was James Watt. The idea in Watt's mind generated an economic process. His thought had economic results for us all. So it is in all things. History starts with individual men, not with movements. Aristotle, not only what he did, but also how he lived, *is* history.

As far as the lower school is concerned, the Waldorf system is in tune with Emerson, who tried to enrich the world through his galaxy of representative men. We, too, must select representative men. If we teach history as biography, we will never present a closed system or a completed and rather meager thought structure to the child. Rather will we give him starting points for later and more detailed inquiries. In this way the teacher can also overcome the problem of specialization. He can freely acknowledge that he does not know everything and can concentrate on those biographies he has found representative for the time in hand. Instead of knowing all about modern India, he prepares the life of Gandhi! Rather than study a welter of European treaties and documents, he follows the life of Napoleon. Instead of an intellectual outline he can create pictures with body to them. The clothes he wore, the chair he sat in, the flowers he picked, the way he enjoyed himself, the fears and loyalties of the character in question—all these become important. The teacher identifies himself with his subject. He acts like a dramatist, and becomes the man. One day he might be Luther or Zwingli, and on the next Ignatius of Loyola. He works with dramatic contrasts, and does not take sides.

Perhaps his biggest problem is the selection of representative men. Here he is left free, although obviously there are principles of selection he must observe. The personalities selected should not all be from one field of human endeavor. He should mix his scientists, artists, thinkers and religious leaders—and not omit the ordinary folk, the craftsmen and laborers. Sometimes he has no choice, as when he encounters a personality who synthesizes the results of a whole age in his being. Dante is a good example of such a man, his "Divine Comedy" being a refined extract and summary of so much of the Middle Ages. In the Egyptian and Greek times previously discussed, many figures leap to mind. A few only are mentioned here as examples: a typical Pharaoh; Imhotep; Amenhotep III and his son Ikhnaton; Tutenkhamon; an Egyptian scientist and scholar being interviewed by a pupil of Pythagoras; Darius—Heracles; Orpheus; Perseus; Theseus; Odysseus; Alcibiades; Socrates; Solon . . . Plato, Aristotle, and Alexander.

Needless to say, to make a historical synthesis around a personality requires both fantasy and artistry on the part of the teacher. In a sense he becomes a pupil of Sir Walter Scott; only he does not invent an extraneous central figure for his drama.

Human beings who call up strong feelings of approbation, or misapprobation, make particularly good subjects. Together with vivid portrayals of stirring events and sketches of difficult destinies, they can help the pupils to see themselves in better perspective. Real problems—another's suffering, another's greatness—all help to counteract egotism. Indeed, a sense for moral judgment and respect for the variety of human endeavor can develop as the drama of lives, each in its unique historic setting, unfolds.

As each life might be regarded as a symptom of a time,

we might call this the symptomatological approach to history teaching. A sequence of such symptomatological lessons would reveal a metamorphosis of consciousness. Metamorphosis is an idea not easily experienced. All too easily the child will appreciate figures of the past in terms of his own age. If we want the child to understand metamorphosis in man, it is good to first introduce him to metamorphosis in nature. For this reason, the natural history period, a botany period, should precede the treatment of ancient civilizations.

Another aid to bring home an experience of time is the following device: The teacher describes a generation, thirty-three years. The children are a little over eleven, and perhaps some of their parents are in their forty-fourth year. They may even have grandparents seventy-seven years old. In this way, the concept of generations becomes more tangible. Next the teacher might ask children to stand in line, as in a relay race. Each child represents a generation. All kinds of games can now be played. For instance, we travel from point A to point B. Today we do it by jet. Thirty-three years ago? Sixty-two years ago? . . . Another way to do the same exercise is for children to jump a step backwards or forwards, each step in space marking one generation. In this way it is soon realized that we would need a line of fifty-nine to reach back beyond the commencement of our era. How many generations away is the first pyramid? . . . One can see how time immediately becomes more real.

Before the child will acquire a sense of time, however, there is one task that has to be performed. The teacher must demonstrate to his pupil that, indeed, there is a point in studying ancient civilizations. The young rightly regard themselves as citizens of the present, and cannot immediately understand why it is necessary to concern oneself with ancient Greece today. When the teacher first demonstrates the living forces that have flowed out of an age, he links the past with the child's experience. When he can point out in the immediate environment what we owe to Rome, what to Greece, etc., he can arouse enthusiasm and interest with little difficulty.

Sometimes our debt to the past can be revealed through language. Thanks to the long succession of philosophers of Greece, a language developed that is marvelous in its lucidity and precision. It possesses an unlimited power of forming compound words and is capable of making the most accurate distinctions. Modern science is full of thousands of Greek derivatives, and every day we coin new words of Greek etymology. While most of these are highly technical, quite a number are processes well-known to the children, or instruments they handle daily. Words like "photography," "lithography," and instruments like the barometer, the microscope and the telephone. Sometimes an adventurous class enjoys some of the more difficult contributions of the Greek language. There can be a certain enjoyment in words that have the fascination of the dinosaur. "Chromolithograph," "ophthalmoscope"—such terms can engender respect and turn the interest to the words that the Greeks themselves coined.

Many of these, like "fancy," "idea," "ecstasy," "pathos" and "sympathy" are indispensable to us. Others reveal the debts we owe to great individuals. A contrast between the kind of words brought into being by Plato with those coined by Aristotle, to mention only one example, can reveal much of value to a class.

The discovery of history in words need not be a dry or superficial thing. This is beautifully demonstrated by Owen Barfield in his fascinating and highly imaginative book, *History in English Words*. He uses a great part of this work to show the *qualitative* difference of the Greek and Latin influence on the mind of the English-speaking world. After a display of carefully selected examples—words of great importance to our way of life—he comes to the following conclusion: "Words which are genuinely of Latin origin—unless they have been especially used at some time to translate the thoughts of Greek writers—are very often concerned with the material outer world, but words of Greek origin are more likely to be landmarks in the world of thoughts and feelings."

Rome had spent herself in building up the external, visible framework on which European civilization was to hang; and this fact, observable in her legacy of language, is even more noticeable in the character and history of that great institution, our common law. Dignified vocables, like "justice," "jurisdiction," "jurisprudence," speak for themselves of the lasting influence of the great Roman conception of *jus*.

The moment we touch on Rome we are already concerning ourselves with the sixth grade curriculum. So, before we enter into other questions of method and touch on high school techniques, let us briefly review the content of classes six, seven and eight. In these years, all the ground covered is translated into terms of biography.

# V

# In Quest of Images from
# Plutarch to Bryant

With Roman times we enter a phase of history that, once the legendary time of the kings is left behind, yields us an ever-growing amount of evidence. The problem now is to find the characteristic and significant. It is just when we are looking for the most fundamental traits of a nation that the stories of its foundation can be most revealing. The mythology that was treasured and that shaped the character and aspirations of the Romans, has a right to be called history by virtue of its effect. But it is truer than history, for in its picture language, the nature of Rome stands revealed.

We hear of the son of Aeneas and Venus who carried Troy's holy-of-holies to Albalonga. There Ascanius, for that was his name, allowed the Palladium to rest. There also, according to Livius, twelve of his descendants became kings before the daughter of the last of these, Rhea Silvia, became a vestal virgin.

But Rhea was not allowed to remain a virginal priestess, for she was raped by Mars, who thus became the father of Romulus and the actual mythological inaugurator of "Romanness." Indeed, the Romans became the

Mars people, even commencing their year with Martius, the month of March.

But it was not one son that was born to Rhea Silvia and Mars, but two: Romulus and Remus, the twins. The two babes were set afloat in a willow basket on the River Tiber. The river overflowed and deposited the basket before the grotto Lupercal. There a she-wolf came to suckle the infants, who were sheltered and brought up by the shepherd Faustulus. An interesting representation of this mighty imaginative picture of the wolf suckling Romulus and Remus can still be seen in the Capitol Museum at Rome. We are reminded of the giant wolf, Fenrir, of Teutonic mythology, who plays a sinister part in the time of the Twilight of the Gods.

Fenrir and an aged giantess brought to birth a whole brood of young wolves. These chased the sun to take possession of it. Long and in vain was their chase. But their strength grew with time. Eventually the wolf reached the sun and extinguished its bright rays, one by one. The orb then took on a blood-red hue and finally disappeared. Winter enveloped the world for years. Snowstorms swept from all points of the horizon. Wars covered the earth. *Brother slew brother and children no longer respected the ties of blood.*

The wolf of mythology has a darkening quality. Romulus and Remus drink in darkness. This enables them to utilize men who have lost their vision of any spiritual light, men who have fallen prey to their own desires—the robbers and thieves who, according to tradition, founded Rome. The myth continues with a Cain-and-Abel-like murder of the younger Remus. But the death of Remus is no sin in the eyes of Romans *because he did not respect the social order.* Society becomes more important than ties of blood. Here in dramatic flashes, we have a story woven around the year 747 B.C. that points to the greatest contribution Rome had to make to our world: the establishment of law. This law was not to be brought into being amidst tranquilly evolved peoples, but amongst debtors, slaves, murderers and other asocial elements.

The legend has its logical continuation in the rape of the Sabine women.

For anyone who is particularly interested in the manner in which so-called mythological history can reveal much of what later comes to pass in recorded history, a study of the seven kings of Rome can be most rewarding. In sequence, these kings create the Roman social organism. The story of each one makes a unique contribution, as Rudolf Steiner pointed out in a lecture given on May 15, 1905 in Berlin.

Imaginative interpretation is of value to the growing child, but if we wish to avoid interpretation and keep within the bounds of what can be proven, we know little other than that through the period of the Republic the name of king was detested by the Romans. We also know Tarquin the Proud, the last of the kings, was of Etruscan origin and his line did go back to the sixth or seventh century B.C. We are not certain of much more.

From the third century the Romans were engaged in constant wars. First they fought in order to protect themselves, and later to gain control of the whole peninsula of Italy.

In *The Western Heritage*, Stewart C. Easton points to two factors that set aside the warfare of the Romans from that of other ancient peoples.

> The secret of the Roman success probably lies in the fact that they never agreed that they had been beaten in all their history. They never were forced to conclude a loser's peace. When they made treaties without winning a war, it was only to resume the war as soon as opportunity permitted . . .
>
> But, perhaps more important than their stubbornness and refusal to admit final defeat, the treaty system invented by the Romans was a crucial element in their success. If any enemy surrendered to the Romans, he could usually expect good terms. The Romans seldom destroyed their enemies. They preferred to make it possible for themselves to live in peace with them afterward. Although treaties existed long prior to the Romans (the most famous early treaty known to us was between Rameses II of Egypt and the Hittites), it was the Romans amongst the ancient peoples who developed the art of treaty-making in the most systematic manner. Already early in the period of the Republic they showed their talent for law and government, that was their conspicuous gift as a people, com-

pensating thereby to a large extent for their lack of almost all the cultural graces we associate with the Greeks.

The Roman learned to identify himself with the state. He was conscious of his own ego as a citizen. He felt himself of value as a personality because he was a member of the state. Nowadays we have lost this intimate personal relationship with the state. The fact that the Roman had it, made his wars an especially moving affair. The sacking of Rome by the Gauls at the end of the fourth century B.C., which threatened to alter the course of history in Italy, consequently made a lasting impression on the Roman mind. On July 18, 390 B.C., only a few miles from Rome, was fought the disastrous battle of the Allia. The defeat of the Romans was complete, and Rome lay at the mercy of the Celts. These commenced a three-day feast, by which time the citizens had put the Capitol in a state of defense. The barbarians sacked the city, but the Capitol remained impregnable. Seven months they besieged it, and then, as suddenly as they had come, they disappeared. Other stories of collective courage abound as the Romans commenced on their path of conquest. There is also no shortage of representative men around whom the teacher can build his lessons. Not all of these need to be Romans. Here are but a few picked out of the many:

Furius Camillus—according to Plutarch; Hannibal and his Alpine journey; Coriolanus; Scipio; Tiberius and

Gaius Gracchus and the commencement of the fight for rights; Sulla; Cicero. Then come such mighty figures as Pompey, Caesar and Crassus.

With Julius and Augustus Caesar we enter into quite a new phase of history. It is not for nothing that Gibbon started his *Decline and Fall of the Roman Empire* with Augustus. For truly the advent of Caesar did not only signify a break with the most cherished tradition of Roman self-government, it also marked a moment of time from which we can see, if we wish to do so, a parting of the ways in the story of human progress.

The road from Romulus to Caesar is the road of the development of the ego. When the victor in the field entered Rome to the sound of trumpets and the odor of incense, he reached beyond the limits of mere man. Beneath the triumphal arch he experienced himself as a man who had become a god. The triumphal arch does not proclaim that a foreign people has been overcome, or that the might of the state has been increased, but that HE has entered into his city. The pomp and discipline of Caesar is a far cry from the undisciplined emotions, the lusts and desires of the founders, which had to be tempered with the experience of centuries.

Julius Caesar and Augustus stand at a climax of history. They can experience more than a hundred million people who live together as a single community, venerating different gods according to their particular ancestry,

but all, at a different level, venerating the emperor of
Rome. For HE has covered the ancient world with a network of solid highways; HE has tamed the earth.

We might say that in Caesar, man had gathered together what was left of the heritage of the Orient and had
concentrated it to the end of gaining a mastery over the
natural world. It seems as if the crisis could be oversimpli-
fied in terms of an ascent into higher states of consciousness on the one hand, and a descent into sub-natural
regions of humanity on the other. Where Rome meets the
central deeds of Christianity, we stand at the crossroads of
this process.

The Caesar cult leads into the decadence of a Nero; the
other path to a further elevation of the highest achievement in Greek thought, the Logos doctrine through the
actions of Paul. Diagrammatically this might be described
as follows:

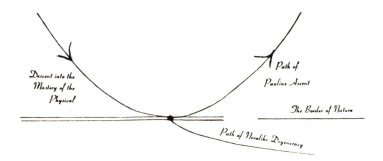

The parallel between Nero and Paul is exact. Emperor Nero's orgies took place between 54 and 68; St. Paul's missionary travels, between 51 and 57. The year 64 saw the first persecution of Christians; in 65, the Gospel according to St. Mark was written. Under the emperor Trajan, the Roman Empire reached its widest limits. At the same time, people commenced to study the Apocalypse.

For almost two hundred years after Augustus had reached the highest peak of unchallanged authority in Rome the empire enjoyed what Pliny the Elder called "the immense majesty of the Roman peace." Minor wars, limited to the frontiers, did take place, but it was a good time for commercial enterprise. Good roads linked the cities and strong navies protected traders from pirates. Law and order helped the merchants. Italy exported clothing and woolen goods, as well as grain, oil and marble. An intoxicating glow of goods moved toward the imperial capital from Spain, Sicily, Gaul, Britain, Dalmatia, Asia Minor, Syria, Judea, Egypt and North Africa. The very affluence contributed to the materialism that would lead to inhuman excesses. But the period began with four able rulers: Trajan, Hadrian, Antonius Pious, and Marcus Aurelius. Only after the death of Aurelius in A.D. 180 does the degenerate Commodus come to power. And Commodus stands at the beginning of the empire's long decline.

Commodus, Caracalla and Elagabalus were all depraved

and unbalanced. Soon the empire was rent by civil war. Adventurers and usurpers followed each other in rapid succession. A demoralized army looted the countryside and a police state was unable to guarantee order. Those in office raided the treasury, and the confidence that encouraged the mighty architecture of Rome was displaced by fear.

William H. McNeil, in *Plagues and Peoples*, reminds us that moral decay speeded social decay and caused epidemic diseases that made a major contribution to the decline of Rome. He writes: "The ravages of armies, and the ruthlessness of rent and fine collectors—great though these certainly were—probably did not damage Mediterranean populations as much as the recurrent outbreaks of disease, for, as usual, disease found fresh scope in the wake of marching armies and fleeing populations." According to McNeil, the parasitic elements of Roman society in the second and third centuries became so top heavy that "a vicious circle thus arose that lasted throughout several centuries, despite some periods of partial stabilization and local population recovery."

Among the great figures the history teacher might select, more deserve consideration than can be mentioned. Time, however, will not even allow the inclusion of all the following.

In the third century there is the mighty Diocletian, a political genius who mastered the art of how to retire; Mani, who developed Manicheism in Persia; and many persecuted Christians. The fourth century includes not only Constantine the Great and the foundation of Constantinople, but also the complex emperor, Julian the Apostate. Invasions became a dominant note for Rome in the fifth century; invasions led by colorful characters like Alaric, king of the Visgoths; Attila, ruler of the Huns; Gaiseric, king of the Vandals. But this is also the century of St. Augustine, of St. Patrick and his mission to Ireland, and of St. Benedict of Narsia, the patriarch of Western monasticism. Then, if we jump to AD 570, we come to the birth of Muhammed, founder of Islam. The teacher is confronted by so many themes of war, like the expansion of Islam, that it is all too easy to forget the doctor, the poet, the teacher, and the general population of the time. Nearly all spheres of life have their towering representative men. Galen of Pergamos (c. 181-200 AD) dominated medicine for the next 1200 years with his teaching. his view of the human body as the vehicle of the soul met with the approval of Christian and Moslem alike in the new age of monotheism. Teachers like Quintillian and poets like Virgil also influenced many centuries.

From Aristotle to Muhammed is a time span and a qualitative range that is more than ample for one main lesson period of four weeks. It is amazing how much can be achieved because of the main lesson. It makes possible concentrated work on consecutive mornings for two hours at a time and makes possible a truly economical way of teaching. Little time is wasted in starting and stopping, and whole-hearted involvement becomes the rule rather than the exception for the student. Just because the experience of such a main lesson is a potent one, it is necessary to continue with another history main lesson block at a later stage of the year, after treating some scientific subjects in between. There is need for one or two more such main lesson periods at later stages of the year, always separated by the treatment of some scientific subjects. It is the teacher's goal to reach the dawn of the scientific age and conclude the work of the sixth grade at the beginning of the fifteenth century.

There are so many cross currents in the medieval world that obviously any curriculum must leave out more than can be touched on. But there are probably at least four themes that should have a place in grade six, even if each one of them can only be drawn together and artistically fashioned within the framework of two or three symptomatic biographies.

The first of these is the contrast between the civilizations of Harun al-Rashid and Charlemagne in the eighth and ninth centuries. A brief list of dates can show how rapid and forceful the encroachment on Europe of the Arab world actually was. Toward the close of the sixth century the condition of Arabia does not seem to have varied in most essentials from that of preceding millennia. A formidable tropical desert of stone and sand sprinkled with oases was the home of many scattered tribes, mostly desert wanderers and Bedouins. Many languages, much restless-

ness, incessant blood feuds, a primitive paganism, and
wealth only in camels—the necessity of the desert was their
lot. Muhammad put an end to all this when in 622 the
emigration of the Moslems to Yathrib was agreed under
oath and effected. Muhammad died on June 8, 632 leaving
a united Arab world intent on expansion behind him. Between 634 and 643, Caliph Omar took Damascus, Jeru-
salem, conquered Mesopotamia, Egypt and Persia. His
successor, Caliph Othman pushed further. In 647—Arabs
conquered Tripoli; 649—Arabs conquered Cyprus; 652—
Arabs raided Syracuse. The murder of Othman did not
stop the growth of the Caliphate. Damascus, the Punjab,
and North Africa were invaded in turn. Armenia fell
under Arab rule. In the eighth century the Arab world
was ready to turn to the West Teutonic tribes, and between 711 and 713 the Visigothic kingdom was over-
thrown. In 782 Constantinople was raided, but by this
time Charlemagne was active, although it would be eigh-
teen years before he became emperor and the division between religious and secular power showed itself in the
Christian world. While his official scribe styled him,
"Lord and Father, King and Priest, the Leader and
Guide of all Christians," Harun al-Rashid established his
fabulous court. The brilliance of Bagdad gave rise to fan-
tasies of luxury and somewhat romanticized impressions
in the "Arabian Nights." Here also two lines of mathematical thought converged, the first from Greek sources
and the second from India. The result was the genesis of

European algebra. '*Al-Jebr*' by al-Khowarizmi was translated by Robert of Chester and much studied by medieval scholars.

The children should become aware of the scientific and cultural impulses brought to Europe from the world of Islam. They should learn how a great part of the Hellenic heritage returned to the Christian West in translations from the Arabic, or in translations into Arabic by Islamic scholars. For as the Arabs occupied territories, they carefully studied those centers of learning that dealt with any scientific conception of the world. In this way they found Greek authors translated into Syriac, a language allied to Arabic. It is to the intense intellectual activity of the court of Bagdad that we owe the Arabic numerals, the zero, the decimal system and algebra, not to mention treatises on virtually all the topics of Hellenistic science, and an Arab culture of poetry and of architecture that also had considerable influence on Europe.

When describing Charlemagne and his court by way of contrast, it would be important to stress that Charlemagne's realm was no state in the modern sense. He was the first of his lords rather than what was later described as a king. Indeed, as he moved from conquest to conquest, he would not have been able to hold his fluid realm together but for the power that was developing in the Church. He harnessed the power of the bishops and used it as a tool. When he took the crown from the hands of Pope Leo III and set it on his own head, he became the forerunner of the later struggle between secular and religious might—the struggle between the emperors and the popes. This was no struggle of the people striving in different directions; they were mere rivals for power. As they both had the same objectives, they form no antithesis. Perhaps if one were to search for a polar phenomenon to the two hierarchical structures of feudalism, one might alight on the organization of the free cities that sprang up all over Europe.

The second theme is second only in time. Probably it is much more important than the first. Once again, treated as a series of movements it would afford substance for a year's study. But expressed in terms of some key biographies, it can be short, lively and stimulating. The area of selection is that of the crusades. The general treatment has been described at length in the seventh seminar.* Since that time we have a wealth of detail provided by magnificent scholarship from men like Runciman. It is easy for the teacher to make the crusades graphic. Many figures lend themselves to biographical treatment. Among the most important of these we might name: Peter the Hermit; Walter the Penniless; Godfrey of Bouillon; Raymond of Toulouse; and Bernard of Clairvaux. Then, of course, there are the two champions symbolic of the strengths and weaknesses of the opposing worlds:

---

*A series of fourteen lectures delivered by Rudolf Steiner (August 21st to September 6, 1919)

Saladin, Sultan of Egypt and Syria, and King Richard I of England, called the Lion-Hearted. By the twelfth century chivalry itself became practically a religious order with its own rules, its own rituals, and its own special codes of behavior.

If we take intentions and aims as a measure of success, the crusades were a failure. They did not achieve what they set out to do. But much changed in the organization of Europe as a result of what had been learned in the East. There were also various economic repercussions most beneficial for Europe. These too need to be interwoven with the selected lives.

Valuable background material, necessary to place selected lives in their proper context, is provided by some treatment of the feudal system. One thought-provoking study of this theme is a justly acclaimed work of historical synthesis, *Feudal Society* by Marc Bloch. His careful investigation of the social ties embodied in vassalage, fealty, personal dependence, and private authority over men, as well as of the older ties of blood, which the feudal system absorbed or replaced, is a mine of information. It is also an exciting attempt to enter the medieval mind. Bloch sees feudalism as a living and vitalizing force in the society of Europe from the ninth to the thirteenth century and gives as much attention to the conditions of life and the mental climate that produced feudalism as to the social and legal relationships it established.

Insight into the religious, political, social and economic

structure of feudal society also helps the student to understand the growth of cities and the role of major cities, like the Paris of Abelard and St. Louis, in the development of European Civilization.

The third theme might be the background of independence, compromise, give-and-take, live and let live, and toleration, which is a part of all English-speaking peoples. This comes to expression in the early history of England. It is important for the children to learn how the values that men formed for themselves in the British Isles by 1200 are a significant part of what is best in our makeup.

The English, a naturally intolerant people, mastered the lesson that they could possess liberty only by allowing it to others. Toleration was not easy to learn. It could never have been learned but for the creed of personal responsibility to which first the Celts of Wales, Ireland and Scotland, and then the Anglo-Saxons of England, were won by the great missionaries of the fifth, sixth and seventh centuries. Without that creed England's history cannot be understood. At its core lay the thesis that every man was created free to choose between good and evil and had a soul of equal value in the eyes of God. ''By this sacredness of individuals,'' wrote Emerson, ''the English have in seven hundred years evolved the principles of freedom.''

These few lines concerning the central impulse of English history are an echo of Sir Arthur Bryant's introduction to his book, *Makers of the Realm*. Sir Arthur has much to offer the Waldorf teacher. His accurate and disciplined pen runs not with ink, but with imagination. He regards history as a pattern of timeless moments, and conjures up image after image.

A treatment of the feudal system would be included in this theme. Some knowledge of the political, social, and economic structure in which the vassal and the lord found themselves is necessary before the transition from country to town can be understood.

Finally, as a possible fourth theme we have those innovators of medieval culture who are a leaven in the historical process that is our heritage. Worthy of special note among these are: Odo, Abbot of Cluny, who formulated a code of discipline for Benedictines; the platonic playwright Roswitha of Gandersheim; the Persian poet Firdansi; the mathematician-philosopher Gerbert of Aurrilac, who became the first French pope as Sylvester II; Berno, Abbot of Reichenan, who made a contribution to medieval musical theory; the great Cistercian, Bernard of Clairvaux; Abelard and Heloise; Thomas à Becket, who like More wedded a heightened consciousness to his conscience; Roger Bacon, the thirteenth-century scientist; Walter von der Vogelweide, the German minnesinger; Francis of Assisi; Marco Polo and the record of his journey to China; and the philosophic bedrock of catholic Christendom, Thomas Aquinas. One quite suitable individual for rounding off the medieval chapter is Dante. The story of his life is much enhanced through the flavor of his autobiographical, *La Vita Nuova,* and his great poem, *The Divina Commedia,* is the cultural summation of an epoch.

It requires much effort to develop images of the story of science in the early middle ages—a predominantly Islamic story. There also is little reason to cover this chapter of Arab culture in depth at this time. For the teacher who wishes to do so, the raw materials needed for study are meticulously recorded in the altogether admirable *Chronology of the Medieval World: 800-1491* by R. L. Story. One of the many values of this compendium of primary sources is that it does not neglect the cultures of Japan and China. The recent general tendency to give more attention to China from 1000 to 1500 is strongly represented in *The Atlas of Medieval Man* by Colin Platt. By depicting chronological parallels in the history of art and architecture, with a stress on art as a language expressive of the spirit of an age, this work will make an appeal to many Waldorf teachers.

# VI

# The Seventh Grade and the
# Calyx of Modern Consciousness

In his *Metamorphosis of Plants*, Goethe describes the life of the higher plant as unfolding in a threefold rhythm of expansion and contraction. First the expansion of the seed into leaf and leaf-bearing shoot; then the contraction into the calyx. This is followed by the expansion into the colored petals, which once more contract into pistil and stamens. Finally he sees the supreme contraction of the idea of the flower back into the seed. When we actually observe how the glory of petals radiates out of a core point in the calyx, we can also gain an artistic impression of how history can move in leaps from moments of crisis. We can also come across moments that take place quietly and then take centuries to flower in all their glory.

The class seven curriculum concerns itself largely with such moments. It deals with less than three hundred years: from 1413 to the seventeenth century. But it is at this time that the calyx developed of that consciousness that is still spreading its petals in the flowering of the twentieth century.

The change was not gradual, and yet a weakening of accepted traditions preceded it in a century of painful preparation.

In *A Distant Mirror*, Barbara Tuchman vividly depicts the dramatic tribulations of the fourteenth century. She almost adopts a Waldorf class teacher methodology for the book by building its historic substance around the fate of a carefully selected individual. Through following the fate of Eguerrand de Coucey VIII, detail after detail adds to the picture of a dying world. The death motif is only in part symbolic. The Black Death of 1348–50, which killed an estimated one-third of the population living between India and Greenland, left its mark on Europe for a hundred years. The still lacerated population of 1440 was also weakened in its religious beliefs. Various efforts to overcome the schism in the Church had failed. Two popes continued. In the weakened condition of faith the Church turned to the suppression of all the dissident movements that were pronounced heretic. Witch-hunting flourished. At the same time, long wars had weakened the nobility and the feudal order. The fourteenth century was a distraught age. The rules of its society were breaking down under the pressure of adverse and violent events. Many of the people of the time, particularly in France, thought they were witnessing the end of the world. In reality they were participating in the decay of one form of human existence to be replaced by another. Rudolf Steiner once said, "In the seventh class the main thing will be to make really comprehensible to the children the kind of life mankind evolved in the fifteenth century and to describe European and extra-European conditions up to the beginning of the seventeenth century."

With great care the teacher describes the fundamental changes that took place in the fifteenth century. These are not external changes alone. They are fundamental changes within men.

The average person today who thinks of the Renaissance immediately thinks of some change in taste. The mind at once turns to Italy, to beautiful and harmonious buildings, murals, sculptures, tapestry, vases and furniture and all those marvelous treasures that have led to an age-long over-estimation of all Italian art. Few will think of the scholarly writings of the period, but those who do are immediately aware that the Renaissance was not an Italian, but a Pan-European movement.

Behind the great "change of taste" there is a much deeper change, namely, the disappearance of the medieval concept of reality and the consequent disintegration of the medieval world picture that was derived from a symbolic vision of creation. Men found a new relationship with the world. They approached nature with what we now call a scientific attitude. This new scientific attitude is well represented by men like Leonardo da Vinci, Erasmus, Copernicus, Mercator, Galileo and a host of others.

In the political sphere the period commences with a child, Joan of Arc, born on the sixth of January, 1412, who ushered in nationalism and the modern age. Most Waldorf school teachers write short plays about some figures in their history lessons. Joan of Arc makes an ideal subject. A full picture of her path and life is a picture of the new age revealed in the light of its sunrise. The danger is to overcrowd the historical canvas by depicting too many characters. There are so many possibilities—Henry IV of France, Lorenzo de'Medici, Henry VII, Henry VIII . . .

While the religious and political forms of Europe begin to crystallize, the process of individualization of people reaches a new climax. We today do not struggle for our religious beliefs with equal intensity. This is only partly because we have grown more tolerant. We have also grown somewhat more indifferent. The children should feel that when Luther said, "To go against conscience is neither right nor safe," he became representative of an age. "Here I stand; I cannot do otherwise; God help me; Amen," can be taken as a motto for the whole calyx of modern consciousness seething with individual power.

Just as the bud has to burst, so Europe had to overflow. Men could not be cramped by the close spiritual and economic restrictions of others. In this way we arrive at the Age of Discovery. In Herman Grimm's life of Michelangelo, we see the glorious pageant of the evolution of Florence. Here the freedom of the individual at all levels stands in the center of much colorful strife. Individuals become so individual that the lure of new worlds and the hope of a fresh start for the courageous fired the imagination of men.

Much of the seventh grade history curriculum is devoted to travel and discovery.

In essence, the voyages and travels of the fifteenth century arose out of a background of theory, growing geographical knowledge and myth. There is no doubt that mythology in particular kindled the impulse that, more than any other, extended the boundaries of the mind.

Perhaps the most important of these myths is that of Prester John. The letters of Prester John are probably the most remarkable of all literary hoaxes. Written about 1170, these mysterious documents were addressed to the Byzantine Emperor, the Pope, and to Frederick Barbarossa. These letters described the orgies and opulence of the Prester's realm without any modesty. This Priest-King John was superior in wealth and power to all the other monarchs of the world. His domains included the three Indias. Europe was informed that a mere four months' journey away, the land of the Amazons and the Brahmins was waiting to be visited. Moreover, it was a country replete with gold and silver and jewels. There the fountain of youth was to be found, as well as the shrine of St. Thomas. There, John himself, the embodiment of Christian virtue and devotion, reigned over seventy-two other kingdoms. For a short time men even mistook Genghis Khan for Prester John. Marco Polo proclaimed with certainty that he reigned in Central Asia. Jordan of Severac placed him definitely in Ethiopia. It became a passion of the great explorers to find this man—a passion shared by Henry the Navigator as well as by Columbus.

Other legends pale beside that of Prester John. But

there is a worldwide network of myth to entice the Rennaissance discoverer. Ethiopia, India, and Cathay, even West Africa and the Atlantic Ocean contribute to this body of stories which, in its illusory fashion promised wealth, power and glory to him that had courage and resourcefulness to seek out phantoms. One cannot overestimate the magnetism of this body of mythology that always lurked somewhere in the mentality of the explorers. History remains silent about the men, and they included popes, who gave such tales active publicity. In the classroom, the teacher must not speculate, but at home he may well wonder whether thoughtful men did not deliberately plant these tales in order to break the bonds of a Europe that had grown emotionally, mentally and socially too compact and rigid.

There is a great qualitative difference between the explorations that commence in Portugal and those that come from Spain. The journeys of the English and the Dutch also have a quite different flavor. These differences can make an interesting basis for discussion in the classroom.

When it comes to literature, without a doubt all have to yield pride of place to Portugal. The chronicles that commence in the later days of Henry the Navigator continue in an unbroken stream to the mid-sixteenth century. England excelled in her own specialty, the collections of voyages, but Portugal seemed more concerned with geographical and factual accuracy. The geographical literature of the Renaissance is given a chapter in an altogether excellent book by Boies Penrose entitled, *Travel and Discovery in the Renaissance, 1420-1620*. This gives a survey of the whole field and, consequently, is much too detailed for the Waldorf teacher from one point of view, and not nearly detailed enough from another. It can, however, help him to select the characters he will make his own. Once selected, extensive research can clothe the dry facts with additional flesh. The choice is great. Henry the Navigator; Diaz; Balboa and the Conquistadores; Magellan; Columbus; Drake; Cortez . . . The list could easily be doubled.

Just in this particular realm of history, there is much good literature. The children of the seventh grade could be encouraged to prepare a sketch of an explorer suggested to them. In this way, the collective work of the class can give a much broader picture of the age of exploration. When the children learn to present journeys and biographies to their own class, there are important incidental gains. Today many boys have little room for fiction. In this way they can overcome their distrust of books. Some may even become avid readers if their minds, like those of their forefathers, are fired by the sagas of true adventure.

# VII

## The Grade Eight Curriculum:
## From Copernicus to the Present

In grade eight, the final grade of a Waldorf elementary school, the teacher goes back in time to the sixteenth century and then builds up a series of pictures leading to modern times with the help of a sequence of biographies depicting major changes in the last four centuries. As the pupil reaches adolescence, it is important that he feels at home in his own culture and has some appreciation of its roots. The emphasis at this time is therefore on developments of western civilization.

It is important that the wealth of material does not prevent the teacher from reaching the present. He may have experienced the Second World War, and may therefore regard it as a major chapter of modern history. But for the young person who was not yet born when the first atomic bomb was dropped in August, 1945, the story of Hitler lacks the immediacy of history of the present.

It is valuable for the pupil to experience how the past reaches into the here and now. He should also become aware of the fact that standing in the present means standing in the midst of many forces acting together. These forces, sometimes called "the stream of history," lead into the future. Future elements implicit in the present are

77

sometimes particularly vivid when living people are studied. The biography of a living person is, of course, unfinished. It enables us to project results of efforts that are not yet realized and makes it possible for us to make tentative footnotes on the future.

Contemporary history is undoubtedly difficult to teach. We are so close in time to the subject that we lack a proper chronological perspective. The excessive availability of materials can make it difficult to see the essential in the multitudinous particulars. Judicious selection is essential.

However careful the selection and potent the methodology, there is much ground to be covered. Most class teachers need three or more main lesson blocks for history in this year.

Considerable variations of subject matter are not unusual in the eighth grade of Waldorf schools. English speaking Waldorf schools located in Britain and America will place more emphasis on their respective national histories. But in addition to such fairly obvious reasons for variety, there are others. Teachers are encouraged to be creative and each one selects his own representative individuals. As the choice is so great, there may well be differences in the curriculum of two adjacent grades in the same school. A stimulating variety of history programs is the result.

Yet, perhaps it is possible to find a discernible pattern that can help to govern the selection of personalities. This pattern has five main topic areas, and the topics can be brought to life via the work of individuals and the panorama of their lives. They are:

1) *The history of Great Britain from the spread of books to the French Revolution*

While it is true that Gutenberg and Fust printed a bible in 1453, it was only in 1492 that bookprinting emerged as a popular profession in England. It caught the imagination of the adventurous who did not have a liking for travel. In the next ten years more than a thousand printing houses were established; 35,000 different works were printed; and about ten million books were sold. When we remember that the population of Britain was less than five million, and Thomas More reckoned that in his day two thirds of it was illiterate, we must marvel at the strength and vitality of a minority culture in which education had become a passion.

The century ending in the civil war produced many important schools and more learning and learned men than any time of equal length in British history. Beginning with More and Tyndale, proceeding through Universalists like John Dee and chroniclers of discoveries like Hakluyt, philosophic innovators like Francis Bacon, and a group of writers who, varied as they are, all incorporate something of the characteristic spirituality of England in their work, the century prepared for a climax of language

and vision. For it was at the turn of the Reformation, between 1551 and 1573, that Spenser, Raleigh, Sidney,
Shakespeare, and Donne were all born.

There were others in the sixteenth and seventeenth centuries who helped to shape the English language, and
some of these giants of language, like Milton or Swift,
might well be included in the picture of the age.

In the political sphere the road from Henry VIII to
William Pitt is abundant with interesting human beings.
Their political dilemmas, and the moral issues with which
they struggled, are part of the articulation of a new social
consciousness. The civil war and Puritan democracy
which followed it may have stifled much art but it released
an energy that called for liberty in religion and most
departments of life. Nevertheless, the overthrow of monarchy and establishment of parliamentary rule was short-
lived and gave way to military dictatorship. Eventually
the revolution expired through faction, but it left behind a
legacy not unimportant for the American and the French
Revolutions.

2) *From absolute monarchy to the French Revolution and Napoleon*
According to Louis XIV, the role of the king was to
decide the destiny of his country and his people. His long
reign (1643–1715) is an interesting example of a secular
and autocratic rule in which the decisions of the king were
absolute. Louis was hardworking, thoughtful and capable.

He did listen to advisors. But he also appointed them, and ultimately made all major decisions. Moreover, he expected them to be carried out. Louis once stated, ''I am firmly committed in the resolution that my edicts shall be observed without exception, since I am committed to them by all sorts of divine and human considerations.'' Unaffected by the beheading of Charles I of England in the sixth year of his reign, Louis claimed, and believed in, the divine right of kings. Earlier, Machiavelli had defied the state; Louis XIV acted out of the conviction that God had imposed on him the obligation to govern. The earth rotates around the sun and society must rotate around Louis. Such thoughts must have been acceptable to many. Without support the ritualistic materialism of the court of Apollo, as the pomp and splendor of Versailles was sometimes called, could not have been maintained so successfully for seven decades without any significant counterforce.

The court of the Sun King, well described by John B. Wolf in his book *Louis XIV*, went through several phases in his 73-year reign but the basic ceremonies remained. Yet, as little as 74 years later impulses arising out of quite another consciousness broke down the doors of the Bastille and led to the French Revolution. The contrast between the cult of the king in the 1680's, during which there was a rising tide of criticism both foreign and domestic, and the mental climate that formally abolished the feudal system and made the National Assembly adopt the Declaration of the Rights of Man in 1779, is stimulating for the adolescent.

Given sufficient time, towering political leaders like Richelieu and Mazarin should be included, partly because they were also princes of the church. The power of the Church had to decline and the rational mind had to be exalted to the level of the divine before Frenchmen were ready for the revolution. Among those significant people who contributed to the change of mental climate, the teacher might include Molière, Voltaire and Rousseau.

Once 1789 is reached the drama is rich with significant and colorful characters. As most of them meet each other, the selection of specific biographies probably will give place to many small sketches. Leaders like Mirabeau, Danton, and Robespierre nevertheless deserve extensive description.

The French Revolution started with a background of great ideals. Its cry for liberty, equality and brotherhood is still meaningful for humanity and is still worthy of study and clarification. Partly through the influence of Rousseau and Voltaire it attempted to create a religion of logic and nature in which organized religion was to be removed and replaced. It was in such a mood that it was proposed to pull down Chartres Cathedral and build in its place a temple of wisdom. The revolution descended into chaos and bloodshed. In the midst of inhuman conditions it proclaimed its charter of materialism. Finally, its quest for political freedom ended in military dictatorship and the unique career of Napoleon.

The Napoleonic wars established a new vision of grandeur in the French. Nationalism and militant patriotism flourished. Nationalism was always a major impulse in the revolution, and it continued to develop under Napoleon. After his final downfall, France found itself, much weakened, in a nineteenth century in which the major revolution was industrial rather than political. The seed-points of change shifted to the British. It follows that this particular chapter of history in the eighth grade could well end with the biography of Napoleon, who died in 1821, the year in which Champollion deciphered Egyptian hieroglyphics using the Rosetta Stone found by Napoleon's soldiers in 1799.

## 3) *The Industrial Revolution*

The phrase "industrial revolution," first made familiar by Arnold Toynbee in his now classic *Lectures on the Industrial Revolution of the Eighteenth Century in England*, suggests a society that makes great use of machinery and conducts its operations in industry and commerce on a large scale. It is a change that transforms agricultural communities into predominently city ones, breaks down traditions and established patterns of life, and of necessity creates an interest in worldwide connections, often at the expense of local interests.

The first industrial revolution took place in England,

and few phases of history have generated as much good writing and scholarship. For a vivid picture of the general background we have *England in the Eighteenth Century* by W. E. H. Lecky, as well as chapters 10 to 16 of G. M. Trevelyn's *Social History*. The cultural background is probed by Basil Wiley in his *The Eighteenth Century Background*, and biographical and autobiographical materials depicting aspects of the period are abundant.

The genesis of the process centered on the production of cotton, steam and steel. Then came problems calling for great engineers. Communications were improved with the help of new canals and bridges. A little later the railways were developed. Among the interesting inventors there were Henry Cort, John Wilkinson and James Watt, John Kay, James Hargreaves, Richard Arkwright, Thomas Newcomen and George Stephenson.

While it is important to study the beginnings, the major application of steam power came in the nineteenth century. Before it ended electricity had been tamed and a new industrial revolution was set in motion.

There was an exhilarating atmosphere of achievement in the industrial revolution which the eighth grade should recapture. It seemed possible to harness and control the forces of nature and gain greater power over materials for the benefit of humanity. The mental climate produced optimism, wealth and creativity; unfortunately it also gave life to greed and inadequate social vision.

It is probably even more important that something of

the sheer evil of the wake of industrialization is also experienced. It was a crude and cruel time. Working conditions were chaotic and a health hazard. In England many children had to work twelve to fourteen hours in the mills. Other children were taught to rob or sold to the Indies. Apprentices had few rights and were sometimes beaten and murdered. Social conflict was the inevitable result of inhuman conditions.

This industrial revolution produced certain results common to all industrial revolutions. Problems related to unemployment, insurance, factory acts, hours of work, wages and workers' rights surfaced in the wake of all subsequent industrial revolutions; such problems are of growing interest to the adolescent who is already considering how he will make his way in an industrialized society.

4) *American history*

When national history can be deferred to the eighth and ninth grades, it becomes possible to give it the in-depth treatment it deserves. New powers of thought are awakening in young people at this time that makes a balanced appreciation of the genesis of America, its past and its mission, possible.

When preparing for the teaching of American history it is useful to consider the positive and baneful aspects of nationalism. It belongs to a healthy human development to experience a healthy nationalism at this time.

*Nationalism* can be defined as the feeling of belonging to a group united by common ties identified with a particular territory. It is this feeling that is wholesome for the adolescent. It is important that the study of the country that provided the possibilities of birth and childhood development engenders gratitude as well as a noble patriotism.

In the mind of a key proponent of nationalism, the Italian patriot Giuseppe Mazzini, the idea of "the nation" was associated with the demand for civil and constitutional liberties, with democracy and with the kind of liberalism that advocated freedom of religion, free enterprise and free trade. For Mazzini the principle of nationality was a noble concept that should lead beyond itself. He saw individual nations as subdivisions of a larger world society that should live together in peace.

For the adolescent, positive social identification with the spirit of a country, grounded in the love of its nature and history, creates the psychological security necessary for reaching out to a more global point of view. Love of country is even more important as an antidote to cynicism, and cynicism is a disorienting evil for a young person.

The experience of American history, taught in a lively and thorough way, can lead to an accurate appreciation of the virtues of a great culture. Without an exposure to biographies illustrating greatness in different spheres of life, young people are more prone to fall prey to the more dubious kind of nationalism, which in the late nineteenth century assumed aggressive and intolerant forms. Negative nationalism feeds on military and economic rivalries. It grows into a political emotion, a powerful rousing force, lacking conceptual clarity. It has stimulated territorial expansion at the expense of other peoples, and entered into a curious union with imperialism. A little later, nationalism became a major force in young nations reacting against imperialsm. Then, in the twentieth century, another varient of nationalism, with a strong emphasis on racial differences, became an essential element in Fascism.

America has sometimes been called a great ethnic melting pot. The whole of its history is a movement toward greater freedoms for the individual. A study of those who shaped the nation can place a bigoted and superficial view of nationalism in its proper perspective. American historical literature is particularly rich in biographies. The most comprehensive biographical encyclopedia is the twenty-two volume *Dictionary of American Biography*. It is much better in quality than the brief Webster's *Biographical Dictionary*. The development of the art of biographical writing in America is usefully described by E. H. O'Neill in his *A History of American Biography, 1800-1935*. Fine indications about independent volumes are included in the *Harvard Guide to American History*, a reference work, profound in scope, pointing to source material on every aspect of the life of the United States.

5) *Contemporary world history*

Communication technology has produced an overwhelming information explosion that makes it difficult to separate the essential from the historically less significant. The closer we come to the present the more we need criteria to help limit the large range of possible subject matters. Three simple questions can help: Is the topic under consideration primarily of local interest or does it have some global relevance? Does the study of the topic contribute to a better understanding of the historical forces at work around the growing person? Will the history lessons answer questions that live in the souls of adolescent persons?

With the above questions in mind a satisfactory treatment of the contemporary world will probably depict problems and life situations leading to insights in four interrelated areas:

1. Matters pertaining to war and peace.
2. Changes in the political life of younger and older nations.
3. Cultural and scientific achievements of the twentieth century and their impact on life in our age.
4. The nature of law, and the study of major constitutional systems existent in the twentieth century.

Each of these areas, when closely examined, will lead the teacher and the class to many problems of a moral, ethical, and religious character. Problems involving values abound in contemporary history, and such issues are given careful attention in a Waldorf school.

# VIII

# History in the High School

The teaching of history in the Waldorf elementary school benefits much from the fact that it is part of the work of the class teacher. The same class teacher introduces *all* the main cognitive subjects from the first through the eighth grade in so-called "main lessons." It is therefore easy for the teacher to integrate historical topics with other disciplines of knowledge whenever this is appropriate. Good Waldorf teachers avoid formal textbooks. The direct interaction with the pupils that they develop provides the flexibility needed for creative and original teaching. The teacher can use his freedom to let history throw light on other subjects.

Steiner encouraged historical work related to other subjects and specifically indicated that history should play its part in the elementary teaching of language arts, biology, physics, crafts, art instruction, eurythmy and music. He also knew the value of asides. Tangential excursions in education, when they are vivid and short, are usually well remembered. It is therefore not surprising that he also encouraged excursions from history into other subjects. For example, he suggested that a treatment of the crusades might well include etymological comments on the word

89

"sofa," as well as a picture of the process of manufacture necessary to make a sofa.

Interdisciplinary work in the elementary school can bring about a harmonious integration of history with other subjects. Between seven and fourteen it is necessary to develop insights into many aspects of the world, and even more necessary to develop a feeling for the unity and wholeness of creation.

The beginning of ninth grade coincides with a change in consciousness that needs to be met by a change in teaching methodology. The mental horizons of the students now expand rapidly, and it is vital that history lessons are permeated by specific knowledge as well as with mature life experience. Above all, the treatment of history must be thought-provoking.

During the high school years a team of specialists teach the main lesson subjects and there is no longer a general class teacher. History becomes the domain of the history teacher. But as history continues to overlap subject boundaries, many other teachers augment the historian's work and help to create a sense for history. With their help historical knowledge slowly but surely can become a binding force that gives cohesion and deeper meaning to the rest of the curriculum, providing the context in time for all that the pupil experiences around him.

Thus, when the science teacher trains powers of observation by insisting on careful descriptions of scientific demonstrations, he may well find additional time to bring in related historical matters so that experiments can be appreciated as part of a time process. The emphasis, however, is not on the history of science. The main focus of attention is on the experiment as a total experience—and every effort is made to let the experiment speak for itself.

Other specialists guide the student through an exposure to the artistic and cultural achievements of mankind. There is, for example, a unique series of main lessons devoted to the arts. Each year has its special emphasis. Painting and sculpture receive careful treatment in class nine. The evolution of poetry and prosody are studied in class ten. The history of music is a significant main lesson in class eleven. The problems and achievements of architecture are part of the main lesson curriculum of the twelfth and last grade.

Already in the early years of the first Waldorf school in Stuttgart, Erich Schwebsch and Ernst Uehli developed a form of instruction for this sequence based on the psychological insights of Rudolf Steiner.

In the second lecture of *The Study of Man*, Steiner drew attention to the process of cognition from two quite different points of view. He first describes a movement from mental images, sometimes called representations, through memory processes to a conceptual content. This path of cognition is like a crystallization process. It is a matter of great consequence for education that this process is one in which the imaginative experience is reduced. A withering, death-like quality accompanies this path of abstracting.

It is through living with and into images and pictures with will-filled attention that the act of experiencing can be infused with a seed-like quality and a sense of future. This process, however, requires a different starting point in the human being. When a will impulse arises from within it reaches a perception not through a neurological pathway but through an organic way that has more to do with the blood than with the nervous system. It is beyond the scope of this chapter to examine the far-reaching nature of Steiner's physiological-psychological learning theory. Let it be enough to say that Steiner develops his thought on several levels and places much emphasis on experience unencumbered by too much theory. He wanted the lessons to be not for the brain alone but for the whole human being.

It is therefore understandable that when Steiner specifically addressed the teacher of history he admonished him to adapt his technique to the needs of the whole child, and to avoid purely theoretical treatments of historical topics.

He suggested that history lessons should begin with a narration of central facts, the bare facts, as they took place in space and time. These facts, however, must be presented with skill and ingenuity so that the listener has an imaginative picture of the facts. He or she must experience these facts in the spirit, see them spread out as a continuous whole in space, and also as part of the process of time.

After this artistic statement of key facts, details concerning the characters or events in the narration are added. In this way the teacher is still keeping the attention on the facts but he is moving from simple narration to a more elaborate description involving the feelings of the students to a much greater extent. These two stages—fundamental exposition and descriptive elaboration—can and should follow each other in the same lesson. Next day, after the lesson has been carried through sleep, the content can be reawakened in a revision involving the class. The thoughts and images of the first lesson are then ready for discussion. It is interesting to observe how far-reaching and penetrating these discussions sometimes prove to be when they take place on the second day. Steiner discouraged superficial immediate reaction to historical thought and encouraged teachers to stimulate students to form their own opinions, and to reflect on their own reactions on the second day. It is excellent when creative work, be it written or artistic, can bring the lesson into a relationship with deeds on a third day. In this way a history lesson can go through a deepening, beginning with an imaginative whole, entering a second phase in which feelings and individual responses predominate, and finally coming to expression in purposeful actions. The time between lessons is a crucial element in this deepening.

Another consideration for the history teacher is the distinction Steiner made between what he termed Epimethean and Promethean modes of history teaching. Epime-

thean history teaching is oriented toward the past and ex-
amines the past in a contemplative manner. Promethean
history teaching is less reflective and emphasizes the
future. In Hesiod and Aeschylus, Prometheus epitomizes
the spirit of revolt against fettering tradition. His very
name means "fire thought" or "fire thinker." His intentions are far reaching. There are always intentions in-
herent in situations and people. When the teacher brings
intentions to life in the classroom, a fiery element makes
itself felt. Thus a discussion of past expressions of democracy, communism and fascism can be Epimethean and
somewhat passive. But as soon as the focus is on the intentions of democracy, communism and fascism, the discussion inevitably leads into projections for the future.
Debate becomes heated and the atmosphere is stimulating. Promethean history teaching awakens interest, enthusiasm and inner activity. The teacher must find the
right balance between these approaches and prepare his
lessons accordingly.

While there is considerable curriculum content flexibility in the Waldorf school, it is fundamentally true to
say that the major topics covered in class eight are once
more introduced in class nine. As Steiner indicated in a
faculty meeting (November 15, 1920), "Take the themes
of the last four centuries as your guiding motif. They
should really be covered in both classes. You should be
able to take it in different ways. In the eighth class move
in the form of a narrative, in the ninth enter more into the

ideas of the last centuries. You would have to make it your aim to bring the leading ideas before the children."

We have examined some of the main features of this development in the last chapter. Obviously, the same themes can be treated with little duplication of illustrative examples. The texture of lessons will be quite different when a biographical-narrative style is used and when those events and thoughts are studied that are central to the widening of man's horizons geographically and astronomically in the fifteenth and sixteenth centuries; to the transition from feudalism and other old social systems to the political associations of the sixteenth and seventeenth centuries, to the impact of the Enlightenment in the seventeenth and eighteenth centuries; to the American, French, and Industrial Revolutions; to the development of science and new views of the world, and to contemporary global and national history.

But Steiner warns that "if one continues the same teaching methods from class nine to class ten without changing their character, then the child's soul will react in an unfavorable way." He made this statement in the first of two lectures on *Education and Adolescence* delivered in Stuttgart on June 21, 1922. It is well worthwhile to reflect on the difference not only between the elementary and the high school, but also within the high school, between classes nine and ten.

Steiner wanted the teachers to explore causal relationships in various ways in classes seven, eight and nine, but not earlier than in the twelfth year of life. In class ten the emphasis is placed strongly on motivation and intention. The challenge to discover the meaning and purposes of historical events is particularly great because the main topic is ancient history. The young person is asked to consider quite other forms of consciousness.

Steiner wanted the teacher to start from historical documents or historical data and then bring forward a comprehensive view of human development through the cultural epochs. In a classic understatement he stressed the strenuous and thorough preparation needed:

> As to history teaching in class ten, it is essential to be well prepared. In the tenth class you would go back to the earliest historical times and from there right through the downfall of the freedom of Greece, arranged in the following way: Oldest Indian time, Persian time, Egypto-Chaldean time, Greek time up till the downfall of Greek freedom, till the battle of Chaeronea in 338 A.D.

If one takes the idea of using original source material from mythology and archaeology seriously the teacher must concern himself with the many problems surrounding questions of historical evidence. Much of the work of the tenth class takes him to pre-history—and therefore to archaeology. Recent work in archaeology is pertinent and deserves consideration. There are also significant problems and uncertainties within the archaeological disciplines that need clarification. One comprehensive and up-to-date survey of archaeological achievements and problems, useful to the high school history teacher, is the *Cambridge Encyclopedia of Archaeology*.

Some schools also emphasize the difference between evidence and interpretation of evidence in the classroom. It is not unimportant for the students to understand how little we actually know with certainty from evidence and how much imagination must add to the facts in order to arrive at the whole story of man's existence on earth.

The tenth grade curriculum ends with the battle of Chaeronea in which Philip, two years before his death, defeats the Greeks thereby setting the world stage for his son Alexander the Great. It has to do with pre-Christian times in which religious experience was quite different. In most cultures many divinities guide the destiny of human beings. The progression of cultures reveals a process of increasing involvement with the earth. The teacher can trace how the human personality can take hold of the earth. The eleventh grade curriculum is not a chronological continuation but a great contrast. It is concerned with some historical aspects of Christianity and its ongoing mysteries.

As Walter Johannes Stein liked to point out, the fifteen- and sixteen-year-old student wishes to stand firmly on the earth. But once sixteen is past, and a certain inner security is reached, the soul opens out once more and seeks pure knowledge which helps to explain the detail in the widest context. The relationship of the particular and the general, the microcosm and the macrocosm, becomes an unconscious need as the soul reaches out to the stars.

If one robs young people of the opportunity to gain worldwide perspectives at sixteen or seventeen, they can easily fall prey to uncontrolled forces of greed and eroticism that arise out of their physiological-psychological constitution.

In the eleventh class, history teaching is related to a main lesson in literature devoted to the medieval epic *Parzival*. As Helen Mustard and Charles Passage have stated in the introduction to their translation of Wolfram von Eschenbach's romance, "The scope of *Parzival* is greater than that of any medieval literary work except Dante's *Divine Comedy*, and in his way Wolfram encompasses as much of human experience as does the Italian poet. His two spheres, the Arthurian circle and the Grail circle, include most of the important aspects of human existence, worldly and spiritual."

The more obvious themes of the poem are the values of the chivalric age, the nature of love, and the quest for the Holy Grail. A more penetrating study reveals the faustian qualities of the *Parzival*. It is probably the first time in western European literature that the inner development of the hero is the central theme. The poem has a modern note because it depicts the psychological problems and possibilities of the modern human being. In that sense it is a prophetic work.

The experience of decades has confirmed that the Parsifal period is frequently remembered by old scholars as a source of inspiration in later life. It can awaken an organ for the recognition of destiny. These are large claims but there is considerable experience and a substantial anthroposophical literature to support them. Related materials can range from Stonehenge and Karnak to nineteenth century works of art like Dostoevsky's *The Idiot*. Among the many valuable books devoted to this main lesson period, two, as yet untranslated, deserve special mention. The first and most fundamental is *Weltgeschichte im Lichte des Heiligen Gral* by Walter Johannes Stein. The second is the recent *Der Gral in Europa* by Gerhard von dem Borne.

Rudolf Steiner preferred that a historical treatment of the Middle Ages in general, and of the ninth to the twelfth centuries in particular, would precede the Parsifal period. He stressed that Waldorf teachers will not succeed in enabling young people to acquire an understanding of Parsifal unless they also gave them a picture of the historical background. Both the literature and the history require a main lesson. Originally they were taught by the same teacher. Today this is not always so.

In class twelve there are two main themes in the history curriculum. Most important is a survey of the whole of history with an emphasis on the development of historical discrimination. At the end of the period the student should have his own written record of essentials and should be able to see history as a process with the eye of the mind. In this survey the concept of causality must acquire life and be individualized. It must be freed from the idea of immediate chronological cause and effect.

The second and related theme is a study of the life cycles of cultures. Steiner's stimulating indications in this area can be augmented by the work of historians like Toynbee.

"You show," he said, "through summarizing the whole picture of history how, let us say in Greece, you find in a certain way antiquity, middle ages, and modern times. The most ancient time, the Homeric time, is antiquity; the time of the great tragedians would be the middle ages; and the time of Platonism and Aristotelianism would be modern times. The same is true of the Roman period. Treat history by showing how these things take their course in the different peoples."

Steiner went on to describe incomplete cultures like the American, which has no beginning, and the Chinese, which has no end. The crowning achievement of a teacher studying cultural cycles would be to enable the students to see how they intersect. Students would then understand how different cultures relate and support each other. They would understand in what sense the human being *is* history.

It is not easy to do justice to the high school curriculum in one chapter because of its complexity. Its rationale has many levels and as the Waldorf school provides a total non-specialist education, relationships with other areas of the curriculum require extensive study. Each main lesson could give birth to a book and some have already generated an extensive literature. All this, however, is for professionals, and we are concerned with an introduction. Nevertheless, it should be remembered that much of the success of high school history teaching will depend on the artistic forming of lessons and on anthroposophical maturity. The teacher does not teach anthroposophical concepts but without an anthroposophical background *and* an anthroposophical inner life he will not be able to move creatively. He will not be able to master the curriculum of the Waldorf high school. Once he does master it there are many possible variations and possibilities not included in this brief description. For this reason, Waldorf schools differ more in their history teaching at the high school level than during the class teacher period.

There are also conferences, which review and augment the curriculum from time to time. The author once had a stimulating conversation about the first edition of this study with Cecil Harwood, a profound historian and a great Waldorf teacher. Harwood thought that the one-page mention of the high school was too short. "Do include more on the high school," he said, "and, when you write it, consider the great changes that have occurred in the last decades. Encourage young teachers to include something of the history of Russia and China." This wise remark is typical of the freedom a mature master Waldorf teacher has. He can recognize what powerful aid lies in Steiner's indications, and at the same time he can be free to make needed changes and additions for the sake of specific classes, or because changing times require them.